Instructor's Manual to Accompany

<u>OUTLOOKS AND INSIGHTS</u>

<u>A Reader for College Writers</u>

Third Edition

Editors

Paul Eschholz
Alfred Rosa

Prepared by

Patricia Paquin

St. Martin's Press
New York

Manufactured in the United States of America.
54321
fedcba

For information, write:
St. Martin's Press, Inc.
175 Fifth Avenue
New York, NY 10010

ISBN: 0-312-03170-x

PREFACE

The purpose of this instructor's manual is to familiarize you with the main features of <u>Outlooks and Insights</u>, Third Edition, and to share with you the concerns we had in mind as we composed the questions following each selection. Our intent is to save you time and not, of course, to try to dictate answers or classroom strategy. We assume that occasionally you will disagree with an interpretation or emphasis of ours, and undoubtedly you will find new ways to use the materials in <u>Outlooks and Insights</u>. We trust, however, that the suggestions here will be useful at least as starting points.

We draw your attention to the opening section of this manual, "Teaching from <u>Outlooks and Insights</u>." We have devised some new features, and some new approaches to familiar features, that we believe make <u>Outlooks and Insights</u>, Third Edition, unusually productive and helpful among currently available composition readers, and in this opening section we explain what they are, where they may be found, and how we use them in our classes.

We are very much interested in hearing from anyone who has suggestions for improving either <u>Outlooks and Insights</u> or this instructor's manual. Please write to us at the Department of English, 315 Old Mill, University of Vermont, Burlington, Vermont 05405.

Paul Eschholz
Alfred Rosa
Patricia Paquin

CONTENTS

TEACHING FROM OUTLOOKS AND INSIGHTS

Outlooks and Insights is a thematic reader designed for use in college writing courses. In this new edition of the book, we have tried to bring you an anthology of the very best essays, short stories, and poems to use with your writing students. The 98 selections in the third edition-- 81 essays, 11 short stories, and 6 poems--are all interest- ing and challenging, yet well within the reach of the aver- age freshman. Fifty-eight of these selections are new to this edition. They represent a careful mix of well known, respected pieces and fresh new selections. All were chosen to stimulate class discussion and to encourage students to write academically sound argumentative essays.

The book is organized in eight thematic sections that take the student from personal experiences and relationships to broader concerns, such as education, work, language, society, and science and technology. Within each thematic section are several focused subsections that highlight important contemporary issues, issues that concern today's students. Here, briefly, is a listing of the topics covered in each thematic section:

1. Private Lives
   Topics: A Sense of Self
            In Pursuit of Happiness
            Turning Points
2. Family and Friends
   Topics: Family Ties
            The Troubled American Family
            What Are Friends?
3. Men and Women
   Topics: Gender Roles
            Men and Women in the Workplace
4. Campus Life
   Topics: The Aims of Education
            Teaching and Testing
            Campus Issues of the 1990s

5. Language in America
   Topics: Media and Advertising
            Prejudice and Sexism
            Language and Propaganda

6. Culture and Pop Culture
   Topics: Culture
            Pop Culture

7. Nature and Science
   Topics: The Abundance of Nature
            The Attack on Nature

8. <u>The Individual and Society</u>
   Topics: Some Classic Statements
            Contemporary Issues
            Illiteracy
            Homelessness
            Abortion
            Civil Disobedience
            The Right to Die

The readings within these topical subsections expose students to a variety of ways of thinking and writing about the
same issue and thereby encourage discussion and debate.
Thus students broaden their outlooks on the subject while at
the same time gaining new insights about the specific issue.

Using "On Reading and Writing"

    "On Reading and Writing," the introductory chapter of
<u>Outlooks and Insights</u>, is designed to offer students well-
grounded, sympathetic, and practical advice on how to become
more active and accurate readers and how to turn what they
read to effective use in their writing. These reasons alone
would be sufficient to make "On Reading and Writing" one of
the first assignments in your course. We think that it is
an excellent way to begin your course for other reasons as
well. You are all too well aware of the varying backgrounds, experiences, abilities, and expectations of the
students who enter your course, and assigning "On Reading
and Writing" early on is one way of putting all of your
students on an equal footing.
    This introductory essay provides students with an ap-
proach to reading essays, short stories, and poems--an
approach which in effect structures the reading process for
them. The first three pages of "On Reading and Writing"
provide basic orientation. They urge students to read not
passively but actively and critically; explain what a freshman anthology is and how it can be used; and while acknowledging that different people respond differently to what
they read, argues that any work (at least among those they
will find in <u>Outlooks and Insights</u>) has a core meaning on
which different people can agree, and it is that core meaning they should seek to discover as they read.
    The following five pages comprise a brief but detailed
course of instruction in critical reading. In "Getting the
Most Out of What You Read," we offer specific guidance in
comprehension, ranging from the most basic of requirements
(such as looking up unfamiliar words in a dictionary) to
subtler ones such as looking for implications and unstated
assumptions. "Some Reading Tips and Techniques" urges at
least two readings of the text, explains how to make annota-
tions, and provides a series of questions that students may
use to test their own understanding of whatever they are
reading.
    By reading and discussing "On Reading and Writing"

students will recognize the value of full comprehension as well as the need to analyze and evaluate what they read. In addition, they will learn how to use the ancillary materials that accompany each selection in <u>Outlooks and Insights</u> and how these materials can help them to develop their capabilities as readers as well as writers. Finally, the introduction, particularly in "Reading George Orwell's 'A Hanging': A Case Study," helps to establish certain realistic expectations among students with regard to some of the writing they will be doing in your course.

The last part of "On Reading and Writing," "Some Notes on Fiction and Poetry," is the briefest possible summary of some basic elements of each genre. It is no comprehensive introduction to literature but rather a sketch of a few distinctive features of stories and poems, designed to give students some points to focus on in case you assign them to write analytical papers on literary works.

Two features which we have found especially useful to emphasize in our classroom discussions of "On Reading and Writing" are the set of questions that appears on page 6 and the case study of Orwell's "A Hanging." The questions are designed to help students focus their attention on the key elements in what they read, and should aid them in achieving a thorough understanding of each selection. These questions are offered as a concise set of all-purpose questions for students, and you should feel free to elaborate on them or to add to them. We have found these questions so useful in our classes that we reprint them here for your convenience:

1. Do I like the essay or not? What, for me, are the most interesting parts of it? What parts do I find least interesting or hardest to understand?

2. What is the essay's main idea? What are the chief supporting ideas, and how do they relate to the main idea?

3. What is the author's attitude toward the essay's subject? What is the author's purpose? What readers was the author apparently writing for, and what is his or her attitude toward them? How am I part of the intended audience--if I am?

4. How is the essay structured? How does its organization relate to its main idea, and to the author's purpose?

5. Can I follow the essay's line of reasoning? Is its logic valid, however complex, or are there mistakes and fallacies? If the reasoning is flawed, how much damage does this do to the essay's effect?

6. Does the author supply enough information to support the essay's ideas, and enough details to make its descriptions precise? Is all of the information relevant and, as far as I know, accurate? Are all of the details convincing? What does the author leave out, and how do these omissions affect my response to the essay?

7. What are the essay's basic, underlying assumptions? Which are stated and which are left unspoken? Are they acceptable, or do I challenge them? If I do, and I am

right, how does this affect the essay's main idea?

8. Do all the elements of the essay relate, directly or indirectly, to its main idea? Can I explain how they relate? If any do not, what other purposes do they serve, if any?

9. Where do I place this essay in the context of my other reading? In the context of my life and thought? What further thoughts, and further reading, does it incite me to? Would I recommend it to anyone else to read? To whom, and why?

All of these questions work best when students try to answer them as fully as they can, remembering and considering many details from the selection to support their answers. Most of the questions are variations on these three basic ones: "What's going on here?" and "Why?" and "How do I feel about it?"

We use "Reading George Orwell's 'A Hanging': A Case Study" in its entirety and encourage you to do likewise. First we have students read "A Hanging" in preparation for class discussion. Students should be encouraged to take notes both during and after their reading. You can then use the reading questions reprinted above to shape and direct the ensuing class discussion. Finally, students have told us that they have profited from a discussion of the three student essays on pp. 14-22. These three essays, each different from the others and from Orwell's, illustrate a few of the many different ways people can respond to their reading and use their responses in their writing. We like to analyze each of the essays with students in class in terms of both content and form; this leads the students to a common understanding of what is expected of them in the course. In order to give you some idea of the kinds of concerns covered in our discussion of each essay, we reprint below "The Disgrace of Man," the first student essay, along with our teaching notes.

The Disgrace of Man	title clearly states writer's theme
George Orwell's "A Hanging" graphically depicts the execution of a prisoner in a way that expresses a universal tragedy. He artfully employs metaphor, personification, and dialogue to indicate man's inhumanity toward other men, and to prompt the reader's sympathy and self-examination.	opening paragraph introduces theme and presents thesis, and establishes a three-part organizational sequence

4

Orwell uses simile and metaphor to show that the prisoner is treated more like an animal than like a human being. The cells of the condemned men, "a row of sheds . . . quite bare within," are "like small animal cages." The wardens grip the prisoner "like men handling a fish." Though they refer to the prisoner as "the man" or "our friend," the other characters view him as less than human. Even his cry resounds like the "tolling of a bell" rather than a human "prayer or cry for help," and after he is dead the superintendent pokes at the body with a stick. These details direct the reader's attention to the lack of human concern for the condemned prisoner.

> Part I: Orwell's use of metaphor
>
> examples
>
> effect upon reader

In contrast, Orwell emphasizes the wrongness of "cutting a life short" by representing the parts of the prisoner's body as taking on human behavior. He describes the lock of hair "dancing" on the man's scalp, his feet "printing themselves" on the gravel, all his organs "toiling away" like a team of laborers at some collective project. In personifying these bodily features, Orwell forces the reader to see the prisoner's vitality, his humanity. The reader, in turn, associates each bodily part with himself; he becomes highly aware of the frailty of life. As the author focuses on how easily these actions can be stopped, in any human being, "with a sudden snap," the reader feels the "wrongness"

> Part II: Orwell's use of personification
>
> examples
>
> effect upon reader

of the hanging as if his own
life were threatened.

In addition to creating
this sense of unmistakable
life, Orwell uses the dog as
a standard for evaluating
the characters' appreciation
of human life. The dog
loves people--he is "wild
with glee to find so many   examples
human beings together"--and
the person he loves the most
is the prisoner, who has
been treated as less than
human by the jail atten-
dants. When the prisoner
starts to pray, the other
people are silent, but the
dog answers "with a whine."
Even after the hanging, the
dog runs directly to the
gallows to see the prisoner
again. The reader is forced
to reflect on his own reac-
tion: Which is more shock-   effect upon reader
ing, the dog's actions or
the observers' cold re-
sponse?

Finally, Orwell refers
to the characters' nationalities to stress that this
insensitivity extends to all
nationalities and races.
The hanging takes place in
Burma, in a jail run by a   examples
European army doctor and a
native of southern India.
The warders are also Indians, and the hangman is actually a fellow prisoner.
The author calls attention
to each of these partici-
pants, and implies that each
of them might have halted
the brutal proceedings. He
was there too and could have
intervened when he suddenly
realized that killing the
prisoner would be wrong.
Yet the "formality of the
hanging" goes on.

As he reflects on the
meaning of suddenly destroying human life, Orwell em-

phasizes the similarities among all men, regardless of nationality. Before the hanging, they are "seeing, hearing, feeling, understanding the same world," and afterward there would be "one mind less, one world less." Such feelings do not affect the other characters, who think of the hanging not as killing but as a job to be done, a job made unpleasant by those reminders (the incident of the dog, the prisoner's praying) that they are dealing with a human being. Orwell uses dialogue to show how selfish and callous the observers are. Though they have different accents--the superintendent's "for God's sake hurry up," the Dravidian's "It was all finished"--they think and feel the same. Their words, such as "<u>He's</u> all right," show that they are more concerned about their own lives than the one they are destroying.

Although George Orwell sets his story in Burma, his point is universal: although he deals with capital punishment, he implies other questions of life and death. We are all faced with issues such as capital punishment, abortion, and euthanasia, and sometimes we find ourselves directly involved, as Orwell did. "A Hanging" urges us to examine ourselves and to take very seriously the value of a human life.

Part III: Orwell's use of dialogue

examples

conclusion

restatement of thesis

After going over this essay with your students you may want to assign the other two essays, "For Capital Punishment" and "Killing for Fun," for them to analyze independently.

Using the Selections in <u>Outlooks and Insights</u>

Each section of <u>Outlooks and Insights</u> begins with a picture and several provocative epigraphs that touch upon the topics of each subsection in the unit. They establish the range of the theme and chart out the territory for students before they begin reading the individual selections.

The picture and epigraphs can be used as the basis for discussion and writing assignments. Most of our epigraphs amount to pithy but unsupported thesis statements and can be developed or rebutted. The pictures may be turned to productive use also. Each photograph can be used for an assignment in description, of course, and some are quite challenging. In addition, each can also evoke memories and emotions, and these in turn can be used by students in writing essays.

We introduce each selection with a biographical headnote that sets the piece in the context of the author's work and supplies information about the author's original audience and purpose. Because of this relationship between a headnote and the selection it introduces, students would do well to read the headnote before proceeding to read the selection itself.

The questions and writing topics supplied for each selection further develop and exploit the advice and instruction given in "On Reading and Writing." The study questions about each essay, story, and poem, like the general questions in the introduction, help students to test and increase their understanding of what they have read, and may also help them gather material for analytical papers. Some questions ask for the selection's thesis, or main idea; others, about specific details within the selection; and still others, about aspects of the selection's organization and style. The Writing Topics suggest a few ways that students may use a reading in their writing or to start them on their own lines of thought.

Students should also be encouraged to read the selections for an understanding and an appreciation of form and technique. And to that end some study questions address such rhetorical considerations as organization, tone, audience, and style in a nontechnical manner. If you want to spend class time working on a particular rhetorical mode (argumentation, for example), you will find our rhetorical table of contents particularly helpful in planning your assignments. (The rhetorical table of contents appears on p. xv of the text and is reprinted on pp. 9-13 of this instructor's manual for your convenience.) Finally, don't forget to point out to your students the glossary of useful literary and rhetorical terms on p. 787 of the text, so that they can consult it when they need to.

Most of this manual is devoted to our notes on the questions--the answers we would give, the way we would handle discussion of the question in class, the points we would look for in a student essay growing out of one of the "Writing Topics." Perhaps you will disagree with our interpretations on occasion, or find your own writing assignments more fitting on occasion. Nonetheless we offer our answers, if only to reveal what we had in mind with our questions, and hope you may find them useful.

Using Outlooks and Insights for Writing

As you can see, Outlooks and Insights offers a variety of materials and ways for students to use them in your writing course. We suggest that you have your students
--write about the picture that appears at the beginning of each section.
--write about one or more of the section epigraphs.
--write analytical essays about the readings. The general questions in "On Reading and Writing" and the specific questions that follow each selection help them get started.
--write essays in response to the "Writing Topics" that follow each reading. These are designed to elicit results ranging from autobiographical essays and arguments to research papers.

Of course, it always makes good pedagogical sense not to give the same type of writing assignment too often to the same class, but to vary their assignments to help develop versatility. And don't overlook one of the richest resources for students seeking to discover ideas for their writing: the classroom discussions you conduct on each reading.

RHETORICAL TABLE OF CONTENTS

ARGUMENT AND PERSUASION

A Sense of Self

SHAME

Dick Gregory

Questions for Study and Discussion (p. 35)

1. Shame for Gregory is his lack of self-respect and
the respect of others, because of his family's poverty and
lack of a father, and his feelings of shame are brought on
by his teacher's revealing those conditions. In paragraph
28 he says, "Now there was shame everywhere. It seemed like
the whole world had been inside that classroom, everyone had
heard what the teacher had said, everyone had turned and
felt sorry for me."
2. Gregory's opinion of his teacher's attitude is
detailed in paragraphs 5 and 6. That attitude is also
expressed by her revealing to the class Gregory's lack of a
father (and her facial expression while so doing--paragraphs
20 and 22) and by her reference to "you and your kind" (20).
Her choosing him to wash blackboards for her (25) made him
think she liked him, but in the context of the story she may
have had another reason; most children detest being kept
after school.
3. Throughout the story, money is a symbol of prestige
which can "buy" attention, respect, and even "a Daddy" (7).
Gregory drops money on Helen's stoop, and he can forget her
only after he is "making money" (3). Gregory's effort to
contribute to the Community Chest is a direct public bid for
respect. In the final incident of the story, Gregory meets
a tramp who has self-respect and is not ashamed of his
poverty.
4. A number of details are mentioned in passing within
the essay: the lack of water and central heat in the apartment (1), the lack of adequate meals and proper food (5,
25), that Gregory had few clothes and no shoes and shared
his bed with five other people (5), and that he shined shoes
and sold newspapers to make extra money (29). We can infer
that the apartment must have been dingy, crowded, hot in
summer and cold in winter, and that Gregory's mother was
harassed and overworked and gave him little attention or
emotional support.
5. The repetition of the words shame and money keep
the story's theme constantly in the foreground. These are
emotionally evocative words, and many students will surely
mention the impact of those words on their feelings. Other
repetitions include pregnant (5) to indicate Gregory's
preoccupation with poverty; Helene and Helene Tucker
(especially in paragraph 3) who is "a symbol of everything

you want" (2); and <u>Daddy</u>, so different in connotation from <u>father</u>.

Writing Topics (p. 35)

1. The purpose of this assignment is to elicit narratives of significant personal experiences, and not necessarily humiliating ones such as Gregory's. "Shame" can nonetheless serve as a good model because it recaptures in precise detail the situation which elicited Gregory's feelings of shame. Similarly, students should be encouraged to show what happened, using as much detail as possible before going on to tell what the incident meant to them then and now.

2. This assignment is like 1 above, but more general in scope. A class discussion of some institutions and organizations (e.g., school and college, church, the Scouts, athletic teams) may suggest possible topics. Such bodies may reward individualism or squelch it, support one's self-esteem or damage it, and so on. The resulting compositions may include narrative but should also analyze cause and effect.

3. Gregory's essay is a vivid example of how dependence on others' approval is no substitute for genuine self-respect. His experience therefore parallels Didion's failure to be chosen for Phi Beta Kappa. Students should also compare Gregory's episode involving the tramp with Didion's examples of self-respect (see, for example, her paragraph 6).

Before beginning to write, students may find it helpful to review the essay and make a list of Didion's perceptions concerning self-respect.

SHOOTING AN ELEPHANT

George Orwell

Questions for Study and Discussion (p. 42)

1. The setting of the story is Lower Burma which, at the time of the incident, was part of Britain's colonial empire. Since Orwell narrates the story in order to illustrate the dynamics of imperialism, the setting is crucial to the story. Orwell writes in his essay about "the hollowness, the futility of the white man's dominion in the East" (7) and observes that "when the white man turns tyrant it is his own freedom he destroys" (7).

2. At the conclusion of the essay Orwell explains that he shot the elephant "solely to avoid looking like a fool." Earlier in paragraph 7 he notes that he did it because the natives expected him to. Some students may wonder, however, whether Orwell was not also afraid of being trampled by the

elephant. He says this is not so (9), but his vivid description of the dead coolie (4) and his awareness of the
physical danger to himself (9) may lead students to read
between the lines. We would say only that the text does not
directly support such an interpretation.

3. In paragraph 5 Orwell states the point of the
story, which is "the hollowness, the utter futility of the
white man's dominion in the East. . . . When the white man
turns tyrant it is his own freedom that he destroys. . . .
In every crisis he has got to do what the 'natives' expect
of him." See also paragraphs 2-3, 7, 9, and 14.

4. At this point you may wish to select various pas-
sages to examine the remarkable detail that Orwell conveys.
The description of the elephant in particular is a master-
piece of diction. Note for instance the elephant's "preoccupied grandmotherly air" (8) and the precise verbs Orwell
chooses. The slowness of the animal's death is captured
through sentence rhythm and structure, for example in the
numerous compound-complex sentences in the section, which
seem to imitate the elephant's prolonged agony.

5. In the final paragraph Orwell presents a series of
rationalizations for the shooting, then sweeps them all away
with his final sentence. His refusal to make excuses for
himself--even to plead that he acted in self-defense--is
typical of Orwell's merciless honesty.

Writing Topics (p. 42)

1. As Orwell's essay demonstrates, a crowd or even a
compact group takes on a larger but less rational presence
than an individual. The followers are apt to react in a
more primitive, unreflective manner than they would as
leaders.

2. The assignment requires students to present a conflict dynamically and to reflect on and analyze the significance of their actions. It may be useful for students to
organize their essay into three parts: a brief beginning in
which they describe their convictions, a middle portion in
which they present the conflict with as much vividness as
possible, analyzing the reasons for and constraints upon
their actions, and finally a discussion of whatever conclusions they have drawn from the incident.

3. It is useful to have a general discussion of imperialism before the students research their topic, as the
word has been used loosely and propagandistically in recent
years. It may also be useful to consider the imperialists'
self-justifications. Some such arguments are that they were
"civilizing" the "heathen," that they were protecting an
internal minority from hostile internal forces, that they
were forwarding the country's economic development, or that
they were protecting the country from other, more pernicious
imperial powers. In their research students may want to
focus upon a particular example of imperialism.

16

HOW IT FEELS TO BE COLORED ME

Zora Neale Hurston

<u>Questions for Study and Discussion (p. 47)</u>

    1. Until Hurston's thirteenth birthday, Southern
Whites and Northerners were different from her in their
habits, not in their color. However, the day she left
Eatonville she entered a world in which she was distin-
guished by her color from the whites around her. Her "colored self" is a member of a race, one among many, "thrown
against a sharp white background," but not tragically so.
"Slavery is the price I paid for civilization, and the
choice was not with me" (7). Her "no race" self rejoices in
Zora, the self who is "merely a fragment of the Great Soul
that surges within the boundaries" (15).
    2. Hurston holds no malice, seeks no revenge; more she
pities the oppressors of her race who can never experience
the exhilaration of the struggle for civilization and recognition that her forebears had. Her attitude suggests a
vital, joyful, generous woman who takes pride in her humanity without the necessity of belittling others. Throughout
the essay she expresses her pleasure in life with her use of
phrases such as: "a born first-nighter" (3), ". . . I wanted
to do them (dance, sing and recite) so much that I needed
bribing to stop" (4), "When I set my hat at a certain angle
and saunter down Seventh Avenue, Harlem City . . ." (14).
    3. The "brown specter" and the "dark ghost" are the
threat to whites of the progress of African-Americans in our
culture. Any knowledge of groups such as the KKK should
convince readers that there are groups of whites who fear
and work against the advancement of people of color.
    4. In her nightclub fantasy, Hurston dresses herself
in the traditional garb of the African native inviting the
reader to feel the excitement and color of her frenzy. By
contrast the white companion is colorless for his lack of
rhythm and appreciation of the music. This distinction may
be fair in the instance she recounts only because Hurston
exhibits an enthusiasm that few people of any color can lay
claim to. However, some students may argue that in all
races there are people of enthusiasm and wild abandon.
    5. Hurston compares people to a bag of assorted items,
junk mixed with treasure. While the exterior is easy to
identify as one color or another, the contents defy differ-
entiation. Her analogy works well in making the simple
point that all people are the same inside since they have
the same maker. She reveals again her generous, all-em-
bracing view of humanity although in practice her vision
does not play itself out.

1. Students may find it easier to approach this topic if they first consider what major differences and/or similarities exist between Gregory's essay and Hurston's essay. Before students begin this essay it may be helpful to review elements of comparison and contrast.

2. As a prewriting discussion you may wish to have the students come up with a list of people who although oppressed seem to maintain a positive self-image. If the list reflects people discriminated against for different reasons, i.e., race, sex, religion, ask the students whether these people have common characteristics. You may also ask students to speculate on what influenced these positive images.

3. As students develop their essays on this topic, they should consider whether they can identify specific social circumstances that might have led to a more positive self-image. They may be able to compare the experiences of another person with the same trait and how their self-image has fared. You may also have them consider how much location has been a factor in their handling of this concern and how others have treated them.

GIMPEL THE FOOL

Isaac Bashevis Singer

Questions for Study and Discussion (p. 60)

1. Gimpel is no fool--he is only unsophisticated and good-natured--but he is often made to seem foolish by the practical jokes of the townspeople and the lies and misconduct of his wife. The rabbi says to Gimpel: "It is written, better to be a fool all your days than for one hour to be evil. You are not a fool. They are the fools. For he who causes his neighbor to feel shame loses Paradise itself" (6). For evidence that Gimpel is not a fool, see paragraphs 5, 7, 13, and 28, where he reveals his awareness of the truth. For his reasons, see paragraph 48: "I resolved that I would always believe what I was told. What's the good of not believing? Today it's your wife you don't believe; tomorrow it's God Himself you won't take stock in." And having so resolved Gimpel does believe, and is "bewildered" (84) when his wife confesses her deceptions.

2. Through paragraph 6 the lies Gimpel is told are fantastic, as if the townspeople are trying to discover whether there is anything Gimpel won't believe. Beginning in paragraph 7, with the introduction of Elka, Gimpel's wife-to-be, the lies are malicious or self-serving efforts to deceive Gimpel, and Elka does most of the lying. Finally the devil tries to deceive Gimpel, telling him that there is no afterlife (94), but the apparition of Elka undeceives

18

him--"They spare you nothing here" (103)--and from that point on Gimpel's life is changed.

3. Gimpel's thievery is not for personal gain but for love of his unspeakable wife. And he undoes his spiteful plan to revenge himself on the villagers when he senses that "everything hung in the balance. A false step now and I'd lose Eternal Life" (104)--a consideration which only he among the characters of the story seems to take seriously.

4. Whether the dreams were actual visions or manifestations of Gimpel's subconscious is the essential choice students are offered here. Gimpel believes that they are visions, but then believing is his keynote. More skeptical readers may believe that the devil is a symbol for Gimpel's anger and desire for revenge, Elka the voice of his conscience.

5. The turning point of the story comes in paragraphs 88-104 with the dreams of the devil and Elka. Those visions convince Gimpel of the reality of "Eternal Life," and he immediately undoes his planned revenge, divides his "hoard" (probably a considerable one--see paragraph 81) among "the" children, and goes out into the world as a beggar, trusting to the hospitality of whoever he encounters and now philosophically reconciled to the existence of deceit: "the longer I lived the more I understood that there were really no lies. . . . Often I heard tales of which I said, 'Now this is a thing that cannot happen.' But before a year had elapsed I heard that it actually had come to pass somewhere" (112). At the end of the story he has achieved mystical wisdom, for he now realizes that the real world "is entirely an imaginary world, but it is only once removed from the true world"--the world to which one goes after death.

6. The theme of Singer's story is the relation between illusion and reality, as embodied in lies and truths in the first part of the story and in the mortal and immortal worlds of its conclusion. The "imaginary world," as indicated in the answer to #5 above, is the world in which we live, and the "true world" is that to which we are transported when we die.

Writing Topics (p. 61)

1. The topic of appearance and reality may lead students to think most readily of lies and cover-ups in public life--the Iran-Contra scandal, for example, or the savings-and-loan scandals that were being uncovered as these words were written. But appearance and reality may diverge just as strikingly in more personal areas, such as the difference between an outsider's view of a relationship and its quality to those involved, or in professional areas such as medicine: a placebo, which only looks like medication, can deceive a patient into feeling better and even sometimes into getting better.

2. The Sermon and "Gimpel the Fool" agree, in the first place, that one's conduct in this world determines

one's fate in the next, and they also agree to some extent on how one should live. Gimpel's mendicant life relates quite directly to this--"Take no thought for your life, what ye shall eat, or what ye shall drink; nor yet for your body, what ye shall put on" (29)--and to this: "Lay up not for yourselves treasures upon earth, where moth and rust doth corrupt, and where thieves break through and steal: but lay up for yourselves treasures in heaven. . . . for where your treasure is, there will your heart be also" (26). Gimpel's attitude, especially his refusal to take revenge, relates to this: "Resist not evil: but whosoever shall smite thee on thy right cheek, turn to him the other also" (17). (Elka and her "brother" smite Gimpel quite often!) Students may discover other correspondences of their own--we like, for example, "Whosoever shall say, Thou fool, shall be in danger of hell fire" (13). There are significant differences too, the most important being that Gimpel's life before his visions, though very economical by modern standards, is not the ascetic life urged by Jesus on his followers. (If any students object to what they see as an attempt to make Gimpel into a Christian, we would answer that to the contrary, the Sermon is an interpretation of Jewish law, and though it is in some respects unorthodox Jesus took care to say: "Think not that I am come to destroy the law, or the prophets; I am not come to destroy, but to fulfill" [12].)

In Pursuit of Happiness

IS EVERYBODY HAPPY?

John Ciardi

Questions for Study and Discussion (p. 66)

1. In paragraph 14 Ciardi states: "Whatever else happiness may be, it is neither in having nor in being, but in becoming. . . . in the pursuit itself, in the meaningful pursuit of what is life-engaging and life-revealing."
Students' responses to this definition may vary, but in our opinion it seems thoughtful and reasonable.
2. In paragraph 3 Ciardi explains that the forces of American commercialism are designed "not to satisfy desires but to create them--and to create them faster than any man's budget can satisfy them." He then supports this generalization with examples in paragraphs 3-6.
3. Most students will probably agree that "happiness," like any abstract term (e.g., democracy, anger, patriotism, friendship, morality, and so forth), is difficult to define.
4. Though Ciardi argues against extremes for both materialistic and spiritual happiness, he also suggests in the last paragraph that a balance between these two should perhaps be tipped in favor of the spiritual.

20

5. The "happiness-market" is the world of American commercialism in which desires are created and efforts are made to sell happiness. In coining this term Ciardi has cheapened the idea of happiness by associating it with money and the marketplace.

6. Ciardi quotes Swift to provide support for his opening statement, demonstrating the difficulty inherent in trying to define and, subsequently, pursue happiness. The Yeats and Frost quotes in paragraph 11 serve a similar purpose, illuminating the first two sentences of the paragraph.

Writing Topics (p. 66)

1. Before starting on this assignment it may be helpful for students to look closely at how Ciardi uses illustrating examples in his essay. They should pay particular attention to the way he balances abstract and concrete diction, and how he uses specific incidents to support general statements. This should help students recognize how there own experiences might be used to formulate general statements about the topic that could provide a context for beginning their essays.

2. Students should be certain of how they define "life-engaging difficulties" before they consider their responses to Ciardi's statement. In fact, you might discuss with them how, exactly, Ciardi uses the term and what he means by it. Your discussion may yield questions not immediately apparent when first reading the essay, and can provide students a deeper context from which to consider this assignment.

3. To stimulate students' awareness of their own understanding of the American Dream, you can have them do a 15-minute freewrite on what they believe the American Dream represents. Then ask for volunteers to share what they have written to discover what varieties of interpretation may exist. This will give students something to react to or against as they begin their essays.

CASHING IN THE COMMONWEAL FOR THE COMMONWHEEL OF FORTUNE

Norman Lear

Questions for Study and Discussion (p. 72)

1. Lear's thesis, that "business has become a fountainhead of values in our society," is stated in the first paragraph.

2. Campbell's idea that the tallest building in a city defines that city's values will appeal to many students as a new and interesting idea, one they have never considered before but one that immediately makes sense. To test its validity they need only consider the central position of the

church in earlier cultures and before that the prominence of
the fortress or the wall around a city when security was the
central concern of a culture.

3. Working for short-term values destroys a person's
sense of posterity. One risks losing not only richer rewards that come with time and patience; one also risks
sacrificing the welfare of one's own children and grandchil-
dren. Shortsightedness is then a mean world view. In business this translates into the sacrificing of quality and
fine workmanship for the sake of quick profits.

4. Lear reminds the reader of the ailing automobile,
steel, and electronics industries. The reader is forced to
face in terms they understand that greed and carelessness
are not only poor values; they are also not profitable.

5. Lear's suggestion that we turn to government for
the solution of our problems may strike some students as odd
or counterproductive. More and more citizens have come to
perceive the government as being itself a business and
therefore bound by the same principles as big business.

6. Lear's contention that an individual be judged
within the confines of his or her values is presented con-
vincingly because Lear never suggests that understanding a
person's behavior excuses that behavior. Having accepted
this premise, the reader then is forced to accept the conclusion which follows, that corrupt individuals operate
within a context of tacit approval for which we all must
share responsibility.

7. The old heroes are selfish, shortsighted, greedy
and hold themselves above the law. The new heroes of the
business world share a desire to do public service. They
are unselfish and concerned with long-term investment in
youth and the future.

8. Many students will no doubt agree that we cannot
continue cashing in our ethics for a spin on the big wheel.
However, as Lear points out, we are the product of our
culture and so many may reason that in a choice between the
quick buck or acting to secure their future, many students
will choose the former.

Writing Topics (p. 72)

1. You may wish to share examples of the essays produced for this assignment to demonstrate the range of perspectives and the variety of supporting evidence that can be
brought to bear on a controversial issue such as society's
moral decay and overextending of its resources. Students
can also select the ones they find most convincing and
explain what elements within each were particularly persuasive.

2. One way for students to approach this topic is to
think of the problems industry and invention have caused
either as products were being introduced or over a period of
time. For example, some inventors are so eager to get their
product on the market that either the product itself or the

22

production of the product is compromised. As students begin to unfold some of these problems, they may begin to formulate ideas for their argument.

SIGHT INTO INSIGHT

Annie Dillard

Questions for Study and Discussion (p. 77)

1. Dillard states that despite her best efforts at seeking out those moments of fascination and wonder she knows exist through nature, it is often simply a matter of chance or accident that they are revealed to her, if they are revealed at all. And though, as she indicates in paragraph 10, she "see[s] only tatters of clearness through a pervading obscurity," she remains committed to the active pursuit of those tatters in the hope of lessening that obscurity.
The significance of Dillard's observations extends beyond our perceptions of the natural world to our being committed also to an awareness of the clear moments we can experience in a world more often "cradled in the swaddling band of darkness." In her view, it is because of such moments that we are able to continually struggle forward.

2. Through the analogy of the hidden penny Dillard suggests that just as those who followed her arrows and scribbled clues were led to the discovery of an anonymous and generous gift, so are we continuously led to small moments of perception in our daily lives, if we allow ourselves the time and patience to be fully conscious of them. And, as Dillard indicates when she asks: "Who gets excited by a mere penny?", even when we do allow ourselves to be led to the treasure of a new discovery, we often do not recognize its value and dismiss it as irrelevant in a world of more concrete and pragmatic concern.
The analogy might seem contrived if it were used simply to illustrate how we can be led to surprising moments of discovery, but Dillard emphasizes that the point of her hidden penny story is that we are often "so malnourished and fatigued that [we] won't stoop to pick up a penny" (2). For this reason, we find her use of the hidden pennies a fresh and effective analogy.

3. Dillard's use of these clichés is both clever and appropriate because, through these tired phrases, she simultaneously makes her point about the fleeting perceptions in nature and illustrates the process of how the senses are dulled to these perceptions. These phrases were once fresh and conveyed lively connotations and images for what they mean, but through being overused have become vague and empty; the process is parallel to how, through saturation, our senses are dulled to moments of meaningful insight.

4. By recommending that we "cultivate a healthy

poverty and simplicity," Dillard is suggesting that we not allow the overwhelming traffic of contemporary life to impede our ability to perceive and appreciate those small but precious moments when we can feel connected to the mystery of the natural world.

5. The examples that Dillard uses are illustrative of the kind of wondrous moments of beauty that occur in nature, usually without anyone witnessing them. The example she develops at length, concerning the red-wing blackbirds that take flight from a seeming invisibility in the Osage orange tree, demonstrates that when these moments are captured it is usually through happenstance and without warning, making them all the more startling, as well as fleeting.

Writing Topics (p. 77)

1. You may wish to suggest that students attempt to incorporate an appropriate analogy into their essays to help convey what the "free gifts" of nature mean to them. If so, first try, as a group, to create alternatives for Dillard's hidden penny analogy that fit the context and meaning of her essay. This will give students a better understanding of what an analogy is and how it fits into an essay before they attempt to develop their own.

2. As a prewriting activity for this topic you can discuss with students how it might be possible to incorporate an awareness of the natural world into even the most urban of environments. In considering this, they many find it easier to envision the specific obstacles that inhibit such an awareness.

SUCCESS IS COUNTED SWEETEST

Emily Dickinson

Questions for Study and Discussion (p. 78)

1. It is more meaningful to think about how sweet success may be if you have never "tasted" it. Those who have it may take it for granted; those who long for it never do. Other abstractions that could be similarly described by Dickinson's poem are love, wealth, and fame.

2. Dickinson's example of the battlefield is both graphic and touching. The example makes it clear that essential to the victory is a sense of what one has risked losing. A rejected lover, a defeated political candidate and a long-distance runner who comes in second all are examples of a similar aching defeat.

3. We hear Dickinson's anguish for the dying man and for all those whose defeat is played to the music of someone else's victory.

24

Writing Topics (p. 78)

1.   As a prewriting assignment you may pair students
up. Have each reveal a particular event from their past
that the other may not have experienced, such as traveling
to an exotic place, having a close family member go through
a life-threatening experience, or having a disease. Then
each partner should write a brief essay on what it would be
like to go through the other's experience. From this they
can determine how hard it may be to speculate on what they
have not experienced, or what they did to sympathize with
their partner's experience. You may also have the students
read some of Elizabeth Barrett Browning's poems to determine
the similarities to Dickinson's work.

2.   After students have completed this assignment you
can share the results with them in regard to the range of
feelings felt before and after. You may find a consistency
in the feelings or you may discover some unique and interesting cases. Whatever the result of your analysis your
discussion can give students a more comprehensive look at
the perceived sweetness of success.

THE STORY OF AN HOUR

Kate Chopin

Questions for Study and Discussion (p. 82)

1.   Mrs. Mallard's friends and relatives believe that
her affection for her husband is so strong that she might
suffer a heart attack at the news of his death. In truth
she experiences a range of feelings from grief to regret to
a sense of great freedom. Chopin clearly demonstrates Mrs.
Mallard's feelings in her description of her physical symp-
toms and her innermost thoughts.

2.   Chopin uses the following words and phrases to
create her sensual expression: "paralyzed inability," "wild
abandonment," "storm of grief," "roomy armchair," "delicious
breath of rain," "whose lines bespoke repression," "her
bosom rose and fell tumultuously," "coursing blood," "exalt-
ed perception," "her fancy was running riot," "feverish tri-
umph," and "goddess of Victory." This language creates an
environment in which the character, the room, and even the
weather combine to paint an emotional picture of the emerg-
ing individual. The language quickens as Mrs. Mallard's
excitement builds.

3.   Mrs. Mallard fights her feelings of joy both from
guilt and the recognition that such feelings are not socially appropriate for a grieving spouse. She realizes that
such independence is not supposed to be desirable to women
of her time.

4.   Sometimes the best way to argue a point is through
subtle example. The narrative form more effectively draws

in the reader through its use of imagery that conveys emotion, tension, immediacy, and surprise. In Chopin's time an essay might have been disregarded as too bold.

5. Chopin wants her readers to consider her heroine as she considers herself, as lacking any other identity than wife to Mr. Mallard, so that we may witness her emergence more powerfully. It is only after she has herself experienced her freedom that we hear her sister call her by name through the door.

6. Irony is conveying something different than the true meaning of a word, phrase or concrete being. The irony of Chopin's story is that Louise died, not from grief at the news of her husband's death, but from disappointment at his being alive.

7. An hour is but a fraction of one's life, yet Louise lived and died a lifetime in that brief time. She was saddened by grief, reborn with hope, and died of disappointment.

Writing Topics (p. 82)

1. In a class discussion you may attempt to discern what students' perceptions of the women's movement are. Obviously, any students who have had experience with marriage will have a different perspective on this topic. After students have finished this assignment, it may be worthwhile to look over the essays with the class to see if there are any differences between those that are merely speculation and those that were based on personal experience, and those written by males and females.

2. This essay may teach the student something about themselves as they take a look at their own relationships. It is important to remind students that they must not only tell, but show, by providing incidents and details to illustrate emotions and what leads to these feelings.

Turning Points

SALVATION

Langston Hughes

Questions for Study and Discussion (p. 87)

1. Langston expects to be saved because his aunt and the other townspeople had built up the expectation during the weeks of preparation for the revival meeting.

In paragraph 3 we see the various appeals made by the preacher, and the preacher's appeals are reinforced by the prayers and songs of the congregation.

2. The various pressures include:
    a. his Auntie Reed
    b. the community
    c. the preacher
    d. the congregation
    e. other children (Westley in particular)
    f. it was getting late
    g. he was the only one who had not been saved
When Langston realizes that "God had not struck Westley dead for taking his name in vain or for lying in the temple" (11), he feigns salvation.

3. He cries because he couldn't tell his aunt that he had lied to everybody in church and that now he didn't believe in Jesus any more.

Auntie Reed thinks that he is crying because the Holy Ghost had come into his life and he had seen Jesus.

The disparity in their views can be attributed to the difference between youth and age, between the literal and the figurative.

4. Hughes presents the paradox of being saved and yet not really being saved.

He startles and interests the reader with the paradox. The reader, wishing to learn how the paradox is resolved, reads on.

5. The third sentence, a typical story opening, serves to introduce the story proper.

6. The short sentence in paragraph 2 is used for emphasis. The preacher's short sentences in paragraph 3 are used to increase tension and suspense. The long sentence in paragraph 15 lends weight and substance to his learning experience.

The short paragraphs (5, 9, and 12) are focal points in the narrative.

7. Hughes shows us the characters of Auntie Reed, the minister, and Westley through their speech.

8. Some of the words Hughes uses to remind us that we are at a revival meeting are <u>sin</u>, <u>mourners' bench</u>, <u>preached</u>, <u>sermon</u>, <u>hell</u>, <u>prayed</u>, <u>Jesus</u>, <u>congregation</u>, <u>wail</u>, and so forth.

Yes, Hughes uses traditional religious figures of speech such as:
    a. "to bring the young lambs to the fold" (1)
    b. "when you were saved you saw a light" (2)
    c. "lower lights are burning" (4)
    d. "all the new young lambs were blessed in the name of God" (14)

9. Hughes italicizes the word for emphasis.

Langston expected literally to see Jesus, whereas his aunt used the word figuratively--that is, "see Jesus in your soul."

1. Before students begin this writing activity, they should review the following aspects of the narrative process: context, selection of details, organization, and point of view.

2. Coming to grips with religious beliefs is just one process where children often find themselves suffering through their difficulties alone as they try to sort out all the conflicting information and emotions. To generate ideas for this writing topic, discuss with students what other issues children generally have to struggle through on their own, and try to establish why these issues are so sensitive. Learning about sex might be a good example with which to begin your discussion.

3. As a prewriting activity for this assignment, have students consider the story lines from movies or television shows they've seen recently and see if they can come up with some good examples of where seemingly trivial events led to important discoveries. Television sit-coms, in particular, frequently use this type of narrative structure. Your analysis of a few examples may help get students started on examples from their own experiences.

ON GOING HOME

Joan Didion

Questions for Study and Discussion (p. 91)

1. By "home" Didion means the place where she grew up, the place where her family lives.
   Her home in the Central Valley of California is home for her but not necessarily for her husband and child.

2. Her attitudes toward her home are contradictory. She is both attracted to it and made uneasy by it.

3. Didion refers to marriage as a "classic betrayal" because her parents and brother now regard her differently; note that her husband is still viewed as an outsider and that she is made to feel uncomfortable for bringing her husband and daughter home.

4. The values that Didion and O'Neill share are foreign to the amateur-topless dancer.

5. Didion gives a detailed list of the various mementos in paragraph 3.
   She feels that family life is filled with tensions that do not flare up into open warfare, that are rarely, if ever, clearly articulated.

6. She recognizes the differences between her generation and her daughter's, the difference between material objects and family memories.
   In her own words Didion says, "I would like to promise her that she will grow up with a sense of her cousins and of

rivers and of her great-grandmother's teacups, would like to
pledge her a picnic on a river with fried chicken and . . .
home for her birthday."
    7. Didion gives us this information in her first para-
graph.
    8. In each instance, the word suggested as a substi-
tute is inferior because it lacks the rich connotative value
of Didion's diction.

Writing Topics (p. 92)

    1. In preparation for their narratives on home, stu-
dents should be advised to reflect on their home life and to
make a list of specific details which they associate with
this life.
    2. In considering these questions, students may find
it helpful to seek out another of Didion's essays from
Slouching Towards Bethlehem--"On Self-Respect." They might
then approach the assignment by comparing or contrasting
their own experiences and conclusions in regard to self-
understanding and self-respect to those of Didion.
    3. Before students begin writing, you may wish to
review with them suggestions for incorporating an extended
definition into an essay. Ralph Waldo Emerson's "The American Scholar" (p. 296) can serve as the focus of such a
review, since it contains many of the elements associated
with a successful definition essay.

ONCE MORE TO THE LAKE

E. B. White

Questions for Study and Discussion (p. 98)

    1. The first three paragraphs set the tone and theme
for the essay. In the first paragraph White notes the
special nature of the Maine lake ("None of us ever thought
there was any place in the world like that lake in Maine")
and contrasts it with the salt water he usually sees. In
the second paragraph White introduces his son, an important
point since the essay largely concerns their relationship.
He also introduces the equally important theme of time: "I
wondered how time would have marred this unique, this holy
spot." In the third paragraph, White gives the dominant
impression of the lake itself, "infinitely remote and prime-
val" to a child's eye but not completely "wild."
    2. Almost everything at the Maine lake remains the
same. The same dragonflies seem to hover around the fishing
rods; the waves and the boat are just the same. There is
even the "same" man bathing with a cake of soap. The tennis
court is unchanged, the store is almost identical, and the
thunder shower is just like the ones White witnessed in his
youth. The changes in the road, the waitresses, and the

motor boats, however, reveal that the times have indeed been changing, particularly the "unfamiliar, nervous sound" of the outboard motors: "This was the note that jarred, the one thing that would sometimes break the illusion and set the years moving" (10).

3. White's identification with his son is prompted by hearing him "sneak quietly out and off along the shore in a boat" (4) just as White used to do as a boy. The identification persists, and in fact forms the core of the essay. For other instances of that identification, see paragraphs 5 and 11. White's identification with his father is not directly alluded to elsewhere, but the intimation of mortality in paragraph 13 surely connects with it. These identifications help to explain White's intense nostalgia and his desire to relive all the old, remembered experiences.

4. White organizes his description of the thunderstorm chronologically, but gives it distinctiveness and a special tone through the metaphor of the "big scene," the "second-act climax" of an old melodrama. Details of the metaphor include the percussion instruments of a pit band and the spectators high in the balcony seats (formerly called "the gods") "grinning and licking their chops" at the spectacle. The metaphor reduces the storm to a stage effect and, by so doing, makes it seem not threatening and awe-inspiring but familiar and friendly, like all of nature at the lake.

5. White's tone is nostalgic, at times lightly humorous and at times lyrical: "Summertime, oh summertime, pattern of life indelible, the fade-proof lake, the woods unshatterable, the pasture with the sweetfern and the juniper forever and ever, summer without end. . . ." (8). A case could be made that the tone is elegiac, for White's surprise and delight that nothing has apparently changed grows out of his knowledge that the world has indeed changed greatly, and he with it.

6. As his son puts on the wet swimming trunks, White, still identifying with him, feels a chill in his own groin, and the sensation shocks him out of his languid reverie and reminds him that many years <u>have</u> passed and have brought him nearer to death. In a sense the entire essay, with its insistence that "the years were a mirage" (5), has been preparing for this final surprise, which is foreshadowed by White's "creepy" feeling at the identification with his father: "I would be in the middle of some simple act, I would be picking up a bait box or laying down a table fork, or I would be saying something, and suddenly it would be not I but my father who was saying the words or making the gesture" (4). This identification reveals the passage of time just as the identification with the son denies it.

Writing Topics (p. 99)

1. The further back in their lives students are able to go in pursuing this exploration, the more they will find that things have changed--not only because more time has

passed, but because they have grown in mind and body. (One of the authors recently returned to the town where he was a boy and discovered that what he remembered as tall buildings were in fact only a few stories high.) And many will be surprised at the tricks their memories have played, rearranging geography and inventing features of buildings or landscapes that do not exist and never did.

2. This question should call forth a good deal of diversity from a class, but many will have rather conventionalized ideas of what a vacation is for. Vacations can have many different purposes: recreation and relaxation, of course, but also the search for one's roots (as in White's essay), the pursuit of a special interest or hobby, self-improvement, the fulfillment of a long-held wish.

3. Students may have some difficulty identifying exactly when they became aware of their own mortality, so you might advise them to do some recollecting of memorable incidents from their pasts to see if the process of remembering leads to a recognition of when this awareness dawned. In the same sense that White writes, "It is strange how much you can remember about places . . . once you allow your mind to return into the grooves which lead back" (2), perhaps an expanding sense of the significance of events and places recalled can also occur.

THE ENDLESS STREETCAR RIDE INTO THE NIGHT, AND
THE TINFOIL NOOSE

Jean Shepherd

Questions for Study and Discussion (p. 105)

1. In paragraph 9, Shepherd explains: "There are about four times in a man's life, or a woman's, too, for that matter, when unexpectantly, from out of the darkness, the blazing carbon lamp, the cosmic searchlight of Truth shines full upon them. It is how we react to those moments that forever seals our fate." He then goes on to state that the episode in the streetcar when he was 14 was one such moment for him.

Shepherd learns, through his date with Junie Jo, that the perception he has of himself is not shared by those around him, that he is, in fact, "a blind date that didn't make it" (49). This is a dawning of the realization that he would inevitably become "eternally part of the accursed, anonymous Audience" (4).

2. Shepherd's narrative begins at paragraph 11. The first 10 paragraphs introduce the context and central premise for which the narrative serves as an illustration.

3. The distinction between "Official people" and "just us" lies in how people respond to moments of deep insight into their characters. Shepherd suggests that those who simply ignore such moments are the ones who rise to

prominence, while "we, the Doomed, caught in the brilliant glare of illumination, see ourselves inescapably for what we are, and from that day on skulk in the weeds, hoping no one else will spot us" (9).

Students' responses to this analysis may vary and they should be encouraged to share their reactions and reasoning.

4. Shepherd's essay seems directed at hose who are part, as he is, of that great, anonymous Audience forever separated from "the Big Ones." Shepherd identifies himself with this group throughout the essay, particularly in his use of the pronouns "us" and "we," as in paragraphs 3 and 4, and in his central illustrating example, where he shows his keen awareness of and empathy for those who cannot help but see themselves for what they are.

5. The narrator's blind date and, more specifically, Junie Jo's "marble statue" response to him on the streetcar, lead to his moment of insight as he looks to the ceiling of the streetcar and notices the "Do You Offend?" sign. That sign triggers his recognition that <u>he</u> is the blind date, not Junie Jo.

6. In its more literal sense, the "tinfoil noose" refers to Shepherd's silky, silvery, hand-painted tie that he prides himself on as he prepares for his date, but which appears ridiculous, "like some crinkly tinfoil noose," after his moment of recognition. A more figurative reading, and the sense in which it is used in the title, is as a description of the feelings of embarrassment and constriction at his moment of truth, of the suffocating awareness that he is looked on as the blind date that didn't make it.

7. Shepherd's description suggests that he was a cocky, awkward, and obnoxious teenager. The "sartorial brilliance" he notes in paragraph 18, of the electric blue sport coat with wide, drooping shoulders and wide lapels, of the flannel slacks that chafed his armpits and grasped his ankles, of the extravagant blood-red snail tie, and of the wavy hair loaded with Greasy Kid Stuff, creates a classic mental image of the nerd who simply tries too hard to be a regular guy.

The personality traits he mentions reinforce this image: the "usual ribald remarks, feckless boasting, and dirty jokes"; his awkward introduction to Junie Jo's father--"I'm here to pick up some girl"; and his obnoxious eagerness to entertain with his "practiced offhand, cynical, cutting, sardonic humor" (33). All in all, Shepherd reveals the type of character that would, indeed, be the blind date that didn't make it.

8. Some of Shepherd's more effective examples of metaphors and similes include:

> "we begin to divide into two streams, all marching together up that long yellow brick road of life, but on opposite sides of the street" (1)

> "doomed to exist as an office boy in the Mail Room of life" (3)

"like a rancid, bitter pill" (7)

"the blazing carbon lamp, the cosmic searchlight of Truth" (9)

"grizzled, hardened tax-paying beetle" (10)

"made of cellophane. You curl easily and everyone can see through you" (10)

"Life was flowing through me in a deep, rich torrent of Castoria . . . the first rocks were just ahead . . . I was about to have my keel ripped out on the reef" (11)

"as though you are alone in a rented rowboat, bailing like mad in the darkness with a leaky bailing can" (11)

"symphony of sartorial brilliance" (18)

"like vast, drooping eaves" (18)

"Pregnant with Girldom" (20)

"like a broken buzz saw" (21)

"this blinding, fantastic, brilliant, screaming blue light. I am spread-eagled in it. There's a pin sticking through my thorax" (42)

"like a bowling ball with laces" (46)

"like some crinkly tinfoil noose" (46)

"The marble statue" (50)

These examples of figurative language establish the tone for the essay. Shepherd's humorous, often bizarre, use of metaphors and similes creates a lighthearted tone, yet the ideas they convey also demonstrate a genuine awareness of an awkward and crucial moment in his life.

Writing Topics (p. 105)

1. As a prewriting activity you can tie in a discussion of study question 3 above with the assignment of this topic. An analysis of how students feel about Shepherd's distinction between "Us and Them" may help them put their own experiences into a perspective that will serve as the focus for their essays.

2. See Writing Topic 1 above. In addition, for class discussion of this topic, you might focus on some examples

of public figures from government, business, and areas of entertainment, to see of you can decide whether they do, in fact, reflect Shepherd's assertion about the insensitivity of "Official people."

THE ROAD NOT TAKEN

Robert Frost

Questions for Study and Discussion (p. 108)

1. In line 8 Frost writes that the speaker chose the grassier and less worn path, perhaps believing it offered a fresher, more adventurous experience. That it was a difficult choice is apparent in lines 2 and 3 when the speaker says, "sorry I could not travel both/And be one traveler." The speaker considers the appearance of each path before choosing, and after deciding, consoles himself with the thought that he has "kept the first for another!" He also recognizes, though, that such returns rarely come to pass.

2. Though the speaker recognizes the importance of his decision and its impact on his life, there is no way for him to know if it was the right decision since he does not know where the other path might have led him.

3. The yellow wood signifies the entire compass of a person's life, and the diverging roads the choices that need to be made at various points within that compass, choices which determine the specific nature of an individual's life.

4. Frost suggests that regardless of the choices made at such turning points, one is always left wondering what might have been, and whether the road chosen was the "right" one.

    Students may have a variety of good examples to offer that illustrate how decisions made at turning points can affect individual fates.

Writing Topics (p. 108)

1. Students should probably recognize how each author attributes significance to specific moments in a person's life, moments which, though seemingly minor or trivial when they occur, come to have profound effects in the future. The major difference between the two works is that while Frost suggests that there is no way of knowing whether the right decision has been made, Hughes conveys a strong sense that he made the wrong decision when he lied about being saved by Jesus.

2. Students should look over the other poems that appear in Outlooks and Insights to help them formulate their opinions about poetry, and perhaps to discover elements they can use to support whatever attitudes they wish to convey in their essays.

3. As a prewriting activity you can discuss with students their decision to attend the college or university in which they are enrolled. Find out what other options were available to them and what implications they might foresee had they chosen any of them. You can also consider whether the possibility of going back and pursuing another path remains open for them, or when, if ever, they think that possibility would no longer be available.

2 / FAMILY AND FRIENDS

Family Ties

OUR SON MARK

S. I. Hayakawa

Questions for Study and Discussion (p. 117)

1. According to the social worker, caring for Mark at home would put a serious strain on the family and deprive the other children of the love they needed. Hayakawa sums up Mark's actual effect upon the family in paragraph 6: "Mark's contentment has been a happy contribution to our family, and the challenge of communicating with him, of doing things we can all enjoy, has drawn the family together. And seeing Mark's communication processes develop in slow motion has taught me much about the process in all children." As a result of taking care of Mark, the Hayakawa children show a general readiness to understand people and are unusually sensitive, patient, and flexible.
2. Hayakawa wrote this essay to persuade his readers that while institutional care may be best for some retarded children, others may be cared for at home to the benefit of the entire family. Underlying this is the more general point that people should be treated as individuals, not as generalizations.
3. Hayakawa says in paragraph 9 that his and his wife's "general semantics" as well as their parental feelings made them aware that the professionals were responding to Mark as a generalization, not as an individual. Moreover, in paragraph 15 Hayakawa notes that his wife was able to recognize a logical flaw in the social worker's question: "Don't your other children live on love too?"
4. The Dark Ages, or Middle Ages, are often cited vaguely as a time of ignorance and superstition, but here the reference is specific: in medieval times the insane and abnormal were almost invariably shut away for life.
5. Hayakawa's insistence that it was almost always easy to be patient with Mark may cause some readers to feel that

he is glossing over difficulties and presenting an unrealis-
tically positive view of caring for a retarded child. His
only qualification of that view is in paragraph 43.

<u>Writing Topics (p. 117)</u>

1. In reporting the expert's advice, the students
should attempt to recall that advice as precisely as possible, as well as indicating any words, attitudes, or gestures
that may have led them to reject that advice. It would be
instructive to review paragraphs 12-18 to see how Hayakawa
manages this.
2. Students will probably need to research this topic
before writing. You might also see if any of your students
have information to offer in regard to Down's syndrome as a
result of their own encounters with it.
3. We have deliberately supplied an unusable thesis
here--that the American family is "in trouble." A discussion of this that leads to some more specific and support-
able theses will give students useful practice with this
essential skill before approaching their assignment.

MY GRANDMOTHER: A RITE OF PASSAGE

Anthony Brandt

<u>Questions for Study and Discussion (p. 124)</u>

1. "Life is savage, then, and even character is inse-
cure," says Brandt in paragraph 14, after witnessing his
grandmother's decline into senility. Yet his mother's
similar degeneration has changed his attitude from initial
bitterness to acceptance and a kind of wisdom (16). His
mother's cheerfulness, despite everything, has helped reconcile him to what has happened to her--and, we can infer from
the last sentences, changed "the color of [his] expectations" (13).
2. In paragraph 1 Brandt writes: "It felt like and
perhaps was the equivalent of a puberty rite: dark, frightening, aboriginal, an obscure emotional exchange between the
old and young." Though watching his grandmother's deterio-
ration indeed initiated Brandt into one of the responsibilities (and terrors) of adulthood, the experience differed
from traditional initiations in that it was solitary, not
collective, and was not a performed rite but an extended
life experience.
3. Brandt's grandmother experiences a "rite of passage" when she becomes senile, as does Brandt's mother. The
family's efforts to ensure that the grandmother was not wak-
ened, the week-end visits to the nursing home, and the
author's ministrations to his mother in the final paragraph
seem almost ritualistic.
4. Brandt's grandmother is senile for slightly more

than a year before she dies, with "a few months" (10) spent
in her own home, six months in Brandt's (12), and somewhat
more than six months in various nursing homes (13). Brandt
says that his grandmother's decline into senility was
"rapid" (11); however, his meticulous depiction of the
changes in her makes the period seem much longer, so that it
seems to encompass his entire childhood.

5. Many students will choose the description of the
grandmother's senility in paragraph 11, which is painfully
graphic. The paragraph begins with a forcefully blunt topic
sentence and proceeds with disturbances in the family's
life. Besides the grotesque details, note the insistent
repetition of the words she and calling. Something of
Brandt's state of mind at the time comes through when he
says he sometimes took 15 minutes to close the garage door
silently so as not to awaken his grandmother.

6. "Sensibilities" here means responsiveness to others' feelings; the transformation of his grandmother from a
loved and loving person to a feared and demanding caricature
of herself is a form of "violence," a "violation" of the
boy's feelings. The words suggest an analogy with rape,
also the perversion of something that normally expresses
loving feelings.

Writing Topics (p. 125)

1. An essential element of this question is describing
the grandparents and their activities to provide support for
general observations and conclusions. In answering the last
part of the question, students might try imagining themselves in turn as children, parents, and grandparents, so
that they may grasp the complex interrelationships involved.

2. Thoughtful students will find that this assignment
juxtaposes a stereotype (their conception of "old age") with
numerous "examples" who don't fit the mold. In fact, apart
from the physiological effects of aging, old people are as
diverse as people of any other age or class. For students
who don't get the point, an exchange of papers and class
discussion should put it across.

MARY WHITE

William Allen White

Questions for Study and Discussion (p. 129)

1. The use of the third person gives the feeling of
general acceptance, not opinion, as the use of first person
does. Obituaries are written in third person and generally
are impersonal, offering only a quick synopsis of the person's life. By his use of the third person, White generous-
ly removes himself from a description of his daughter in

terms of his loss, thus allowing her to emerge as an individual in the world.

2.   White describes his daughter picking up carloads of
people during her daily excursions, but never having a
party, helping out at the county home, trying to get "a
restroom for the colored girls at school," and joining the
Congregational Church without consulting her parents. These
examples demonstrate Mary's selfless, humanistic qualities
as well as her independent nature. The diction White uses
emphasizes Mary's generous nature.

3.   Mary lived life vigorously, never taking it for
granted and always finding time to help others.

4.   White shows his deep love for his daughter through
examples and vivid description that compel the reader to
share his feelings.

5.   Mary was a well-to-do girl who lived in a small
town populated by rich and poor alike in the early part of
this century.

6.   In some ways Mary White is the typical teenager,
exuberant and energetic. It is perhaps in her concern for
others and her strong sense of herself that she stands
apart, as she would in any age group. Students may evaluate
for themselves the extent to which they identify with her.

Writing Topics (p. 130)

1.   The student should begin by listing the characteristics of his or her subject. The student should distinguish between traits she/he likes and the traits she/he
admires, and choose examples that demonstrate each. The
student should be reminded that diction is important in
conveying the intended impression. For a brief discussion
of this they may refer to the Glossary under DICTION.

2.   After the students have finished this assignment,
you may want to test the effectiveness of the writing by
reading aloud each essay and have the class guess who the
essay is describing. By telling the students beforehand,
they may be sure not to use their name, or share the essay
with others in the class.

A WORN PATH

Eudora Welty

Questions for Study and Discussion (p. 138)

1.   Phoenix is going to the hospital there to obtain
medicine for her grandson's throat, which had been burned
two or three years previously when he swallowed lye (91).
She tells nobody the nature of her journey; one of the
nurses at the hospital knows why she has come and asks about
her grandson. Phoenix has been so preoccupied with walking
the journey that she forgot her purpose (paragraph 90).

2. Along the way Phoenix encounters a long uphill path, a thorn bush, a log across a creek, a barbed wire fence, a "maze" in the woods, a scarecrow which she mistakes for a ghost, an alligator swamp, a black dog, a deep ditch, a hunter who points a gun at her, and, finally, the bewildering city. She overcomes each with determination, dignity, and good humor, talking to herself for moral support. See, for example, her reaction to the thorn bush in paragraph 8. Her indomitable nature is suggested by her name, Phoenix, evoking the mythical bird that lives five hundred years and then is reborn from its own ashes.

3. Phoenix recovers the first nickel after it dropped from the hunter's pocket (49, 54) and craftily coaxes the second one from the hospital nurse (99). She plans to use the money to buy a paper windmill for her grandson for Christmas (103). The gift, like Phoenix's journey, reveals the depth of her self-sacrificing love for the boy.

4. Phoenix and her grandson depend upon each other for survival. The grandson needs the medicine Phoenix pursues in her treks to Natchez, while Phoenix's life rests on the fulfillment of this mission. Both roles contribute to the sustaining bond of love between them.

5. The Surrender is the end of the Civil war. Phoenix Jackson evidently grew up as a slave, and slaves did not have the opportunity to go to school.

6. In paragraph 1 Welty describes Phoenix as swaying from side to side "with the balanced heaviness and lightness of a pendulum in a grandfather clock." Her wrinkled skin looks "as though a whole little tree stood in the middle of her forehead" (2); she climbs the hill "like a baby trying to climb steps" (16) and lies on her back "like a June bug waiting to be turned over" (39). Taken together these images suggest that old Phoenix is like a force of nature, enduring and indomitable.

7. Literally, the title refers to the path Phoenix has walked again and again to Natchez. The larger significance is best suggested by Welty herself in paragraph 10 of the essay "'Is Phoenix Jackson's Grandson Really Dead?'": "What I hoped would come clear was that in the whole surround of this story, the world it threads through, the only certain thing at all is the worn path. The habit of love cuts through confusion and stumbles or contrives its way out of difficulty, it remembers the way even when it forgets, for a dumbfounded moment, its reason for being. The path is the thing that matters." This would be an appropriate point at which to discuss Welty's comments in that essay on the overall meaning of her story.

8. Welty has written an essay on this subject entitled "Is Phoenix Jackson's Grandson Really Dead?" In paragraph 6 of that essay Welty sums up her answer: "To the question 'Is the grandson really dead?' I could reply that it doesn't make any difference. I could also say that I did not make him up in order to let him play a trick on Phoenix. But my best answer would be: 'Phoenix is alive!'" The

point of the story then turns not upon the fate of the grandson but upon Phoenix's journey itself, as the rest of Welty's essay makes clear. Many readers seem to feel that Phoenix's refusal to believe that her grandson is dead would emphasize her indomitable spirit. Phoenix's puzzling silence after the hospital nurse asks why she has come leads some readers to speculate that Phoenix may have for a moment remembered the grandson's death, instead of having simply forgotten the reason for her errand. In addition the somewhat allegorical quality of the story may prompt readers to search for deeper meanings. But in fact the story does not provide any basis for such an interpretation.

Writing Topics (p. 138)

1. The descriptions should not only convey as exact a picture as possible but should create a clear dominant impression. Students should use precise language and, where appropriate, figurative language. Welty's story is a stimulating and usable model.
2. Preparation for this exercise should include consideration of both general obligations--those all fathers, mothers, or children share--and the particulars of each student's situation. The underlying topic here is the nature of responsibility and its sources in individuals and groups.
3. Students usually enjoy reading more of Welty. In reading other stories and essays by Welty they will find that her treatment of Phoenix Jackson is typical of her sympathetic, appreciative, and accurate treatment of African-American people throughout her work.

The Troubled American Family

CAN THE AMERICAN FAMILY SURVIVE?

Margaret Mead

Questions for Study and Discussion (p. 150)

1. In paragraph 3 Mead states that "very young couples, the poorly educated, those with few skills and a low income, [and] Blacks and members of other minority groups" are more prone to breakdowns within the family. The communication and economic pressures commonly associated with these groups creates instability in relationships and often leads to divorce.

The effect of this breakdown on children of "secure" families is stated in paragraph 4: "How can children feel secure when their friends in other families so like their own are conspicuously lost and unhappy?"
2. Mead outlines the consequences of family breakdown

in paragraphs 12-20. The effects on adults include: 1) large numbers of young couples repudiating or delaying marriage and simply living together, "dependent on their private, personal commitment to each other for the survival of their relationship" (12); 2) growing numbers of men and women "who have outlived their slender family relationships" and are forced to depend on public institutions (13); 3) increasing demands that women join the working force, not always out of a desire to do so, but because they <u>must</u> to survive economically (14).

The effect on children is even more desperate, according to Mead: 1) large numbers of adolescent runaways, particularly young girls (17); 2) children "discovering the obliterating effects of alcohol" (18); 3) young girls and boys wandering the streets, often falling victim to "corruption and sordid sex" (18); 4) a "vast increase in child abuse" (19).

3. The most alarming symptom of family trouble, in Mead's view, is the "vast increase in child abuse" (19). She believes "that frantic mothers and fathers, stepparents or the temporary mates of parents turn on the children they do not know how to care for, and beat them--often in a desperate, inarticulate hope that someone will hear their cries and somehow bring help" (19).

4. The following explanations for the breakdown of family life are offered in the essay:

1) the movement from rural areas and small towns to the big cities, and the movement from one part of the country to another
2) the effect of unemployment and underemployment among minority groups
3) the generation gap
4) failure to provide for children and young people "whom we do not succeed in educating, who are in deep trouble and who may be totally abandoned" (25)
5) the problem of hard drugs
6) parental permissiveness and lack of discipline
7) Women's Liberation

Students' responses to these explanations will vary. As you discuss them, you may also wish to find out their reactions to the "panaceas" mentioned in paragraphs 29 and 30.

5. Mead does <u>not</u> advocate returning to the past. Instead, she explains that <u>looking</u> to the past "can provide us only with a base for judging what threatens sound family life and for considering whether our social planning is realistic and inclusive enough" (39). In acting thus, Mead believes we will be better able to find "new solutions in keeping with our deepest human needs" (39).

6. Mead's concern in this statement is that we have tried too hard to isolate individual families from the community at large and, as a result, have encouraged the

separation of generations and the break from a sense of home community. This has placed a much larger burden on every small family because they have taken over responsibilities formerly shared within three generations and the community.

7. Mead begins her discussion of possible solutions by stating: "Both optimism and action are needed." She then offers the following:

1) support Federal legislation intended to help provide for families in need

2) support Federal programs for daycare and after school care; for centers for the elderly where they won't be isolated; for housing for young families and older people so they can interact; for a national health program; and for "family impact" requirements on Government agency policies

3) realize that "problems related to family life and community life . . . are interlocked" and that "we need awareness of detail combined with concern for the whole, and a wise use of tax dollars to accomplish our aims" (50)

4) accept the idea that each of us "shares in the responsibility for everyone" (51)

5) support communities where there is housing for three generations, for the fortunate and unfortunate, and for people of many backgrounds (52)

6) "interrupt the runaway belief that marriages must fail, that parents and children can't help but be out of communication, that the family as an institution is altogether in disarray" through nationwide discussion (53)

There can be extensive class discussion on any of these proposed solutions.

Mead does not see the dissolution of the family structure as an easier solution simply because there are still far more successful marriages and child-parent relationships than there are failures.

8. By dividing her introduction into five paragraphs, Mead helps delineate between the separate ideas discussed in them. The bold print subheading--THE GRIM PICTURE--then identifies the start of the body of the essay for readers. Though combining paragraphs 1-5 into one may have created a better sense of introduction, it would also have jumbled the ideas together, making them less distinguishable and, ultimately, less effective in introducing what follows.

Writing Topics (p. 151)

1. An in-depth discussion of study questions 4 and 7 above may lead students to consider some more innovative alternatives to the family as the central social unit in our society. You can also look at the alternatives mentioned in

42

paragraph 29 of the essay and explore the possibilities of each in more detail.

2. It may be interesting to discuss, as a class, the extent to which students' families have been isolated from the interaction of generations, as well as from the larger society. Find out if there is any evidence, in students' experiences, that the single family unit has taken on the responsibilities "once shared within three generations and among a large number of people--the nurturing of small children, the emergence of adolescents into adulthood, the care of the sick and disabled and the protection of the aged" (42). Your discussion may also help students draw conclusions about the importance of their families in their own lives.

THE FALTERING FAMILY

George Gallup, Jr.

Questions for Study and Discussion (p. 159)

1. By choosing an anecdote with children as the subject, Gallup presents the urgency of the problem he describes in the group that is most likely to inspire sympathy from his readers. Then Gallup extends his sense of urgency toward his subject by showing how it affects members of the family in particular and society in general. His sense of urgency is most dramatic when he makes his grim prediction that soon our children will be raised by the community and institutions.

2. While the feminist movement has encouraged many women to enter or re-enter the workforce by choice, the economic necessities of our society have also made it **necessary** for many women to work. According to Gallup, even if the economy improves, many women will choose to remain in the workforce.

3. The belief that child care and housework are no longer solely "women's work" has spread throughout our culture. More families now have both parents working outside of the home and children in day-care centers. Although this may lessen the strain on parents, it breaks down family bonds by absenting the parents from their child's growth stages.

4. According to Gallup, the counterforces driving the family back together are a majority of American women wanting marriage and children and the attitude of teenagers that divorce is too easy to obtain. Many students may point out that these forces are not as strong as the destabilizing forces. Many teenagers oppose divorce because they do not want their parents to divorce or because they are products of divorced households. They may react differently when faced with the same choice in their own marriages. Also,

43

many women desire a career as strongly or more strongly than they do marriage.

5. Alternative lifestyles permit a wider range of choices for couples than marriage and child-bearing and may dilute the perceived importance of "traditional values." Attitudes toward sexual conduct have "loosened, straining marital bonds." The economy has forced many women into the work force taking parents away from their children. The feminist philosophy has affected attitudes about housework, spousal responsibility, and marriage. These forces, in Gallup's opinion, work against the traditional idea of the family to the detriment of society.

6. Gallup uses information from Gallup and other polls, studies by the <u>New York Times</u> and other newspapers, surveys done by the National Center of Health Statistics, and quotes from a psychiatrist, an economist, and other professionals, and personal accounts by husbands and wives. Whereas statistics can be construed as misleading, quotes are the actual words and opinions of "real people," and so are perceived as more effective.

7. Both teenagers and adults are concerned with the high rate of divorce and the fact that a divorce is so easy to obtain. They are concerned that marriages are not lasting and want something better for themselves. Yet most agree that it is better to divorce if a couple does not get along. Teenagers and adults also realize the problems families are facing, but few seem to recognize the need to strengthen family relationships as a solution.

Writing Topics (p. 159)

1. As a prewriting activity, you may have students discuss their feelings on this subject and list the ways to achieve a stronger family. If it is determined that this may not be possible without sacrificing the needs of the individual, have the students consider this in their essay.

2. After the students have completed the assignment you may want to share the results with the class. Do the effects correlate? I.e., students who have chosen an "alternative" lifestyle will comment on how their family is affected. Do the students who are in the family cite the same effects, or are they different?

HOMOSEXUALITY: ONE FAMILY'S AFFAIR

Michael Reese and Pamela Abramson

Questions for Study and Discussion (p. 167)

1. Kelly's parents did not "know" their son because they could only imagine what his lifestyle consisted of. For them "knowing" their son included certain expectations

for his future (with a wife and children and a traditional lifestyle).

2. The stereotypes of homosexual men led Kelly to believe that if he were himself homosexual, he had to be perverted, limp-wristed, and effeminate. Kelly was not these things and so was unsure of his own sexuality. All he was sure of was that he did not like girls, "faggot" jokes, or post-game drinking. Having no positive gay role models in his life he could not acknowledge his homosexuality.

3. Gay men, as Kelly first perceived, were pornographic, effeminate and perverted--aging drag queens. When he finally went to a gay bar he realized they were "average Joes," not physically different than heterosexuals, and that they had families, careers, and everyday lives.

4. Kelly strove to be a perfectionist so that no one would be able to find fault with him. He was a teacher's pet, good at football and a member of many social groups.

5. All the members of the family asked themselves, "Why Kelly?" Kelly doesn't have the answer, as his parents thought he would, nor did he choose his lifestyle. Everyone, including Kelly, felt horror at his homosexuality. Kelly's parents also experienced guilt over what they must have "done wrong" in raising him. Joan read books and joined support groups in an attempt to get closer to the situation and make sense of it. Paul said he accepts it, but has opted for mental storming over participation in parent support groups. He said he realizes he cannot turn his back on his son whatever Kelly's sexual orientation. Kelly made the decision to express his real feelings rather than suppress them. At first he kept his distance from his family, now he lets his parents into his life in hopes that the more it becomes a reality for them, the more they will be able to accept it. Kelly is doing what he needs to and it seems to be working as his father is finally a part of his life again. Each member of the family seems to be doing the best they can.

6. The authors have stayed neutral in reporting telling the story of the family. When referring to Joan or Paul, the authors do not condemn their initial horror or praise their acceptance of their son, but see both as inevitable. They acknowledge that the situation is equally difficult for Kelly, who is dealing with trying to express his sexuality and at the same time gain acceptance from his family.

7. The Chronisters ask themselves, "Why my son?" "Where did we go wrong?" "What made him like this?" "What's going to happen to [him]?" "What kind of a life will [he] have?" The authors do not try to answer questions of why or how, because they want to show the futility of such questions. They emphasize the future rather than the past: his parents' coping strategies, the evolution of Kelly's identity as a gay man, and his concerns for his future.

1. As a prewriting activity you may conduct a discussion which characterizes each of the family members. Have the students share their perceptions of each member. Once the characterizations have been made students may find it easier to determine why a particular family member is more sympathetic.

2. It may be important for students to describe the emotion they would feel working up the nerve to tell their parents and the emotions their parents would feel rather than just present a narrative.

SEPARATING

John Updike

Questions for Study and Discussion (p. 177)

1. The majority of Richard's actions comprise fixing things around the house and "battening down the hatches" before he leaves. Richard even makes reference to his handiness and his son John's being the only one able to help with odd jobs. Richard Sr. sees himself as dutiful in taking on the task of telling the two boys about the divorce, driving into town to pick Dickie up and for "putting his house in order" before he leaves. Young readers who have themselves experienced the pain of their family's breakup may not be as sympathetic to Richard as older readers will be.

2. The other woman is not the "real" reason for the separation, a fact made apparent by the author's slim references to her. Rather, the author shows us the family dynamics, which, although they follow the breakup, may give us clues as to the real problems in the family.

3. Each child clearly has a different personality and is at a different stage of maturity. Judith is mature and worldly, evidenced not only by her recent solo trip to Europe, but also by her calm response to the announcement of the coming separation, and her taking over of her mother's duties. John is still a young boy, as is apparent in his dinner-time antics. Dickie is a teenager, cool and detached, who does not want his family to see his emotion even though he is hurt and really wants to know "why?" Margaret is also young and immature, as is clear by her not keeping the secret that her mother asked her to keep.

4. The fact that the windows are closed and this well-to-do family has no tan well into the season, when most of their neighbors and friends are pool side and court side, is a clue that the family is in crisis. Richard's attitude towards Joan in paragraph seven indicates that he sees her as a controlling nag. While John and Richard are outside, Richard makes reference to John being the only one to help

46

him around the house. Richard's tone shows that he is tired of being depended on for everything, especially since he does not feel his efforts are appreciated. Joan seems to feel as though she has been undeservedly maligned when in fact she should be commended for not telling the children about the "other woman."

5. Although students will come from varied backgrounds, most will be able to see some similarity between their family and the Maple family. Our students usually point to paragraphs 4, 13, 23-29, and 51-67 when discussing interactions within the Maple family.

6. Judith thinks a separation is ridiculous, saying, "You should either live together or get divorced." She doesn't even suspect that another person could be involved with one of her parents. John is having a hard time at school and sees this as another in his long line of problems. He also feels that his parents do not love him, but that he and the other children were just "little things [they] had." Dickie wants to know "why?" He wants to know what led to the separation rather than what will come after it. No doubt, like many children facing this family tragedy, he feels that if he can understand it better, maybe he'll be able to undo it. There are many answers to the question, "what if. . . ." If the children had not been a factor, Joan and Richard may have had more time for their relationship and the separation may not have happened. On the other hand, if separation was inevitable, no doubt concern for the children prolonged the agony for the parents.

7. Richard never really admits to other members of the family that there is another woman. Perhaps if his children had known, they would have sided with their mother. However, the author wants us to see that whatever his relationship with the other woman, more than likely it was a catalyst and not a cause for the break-up of the marriage.

Writing Topics (p. 177)

1. Obviously, students who have had experience with divorce of their own or their parents may have a different perspective than those never exposed to it. After the assignment, you may want to divide the students' essays into these three groups, those by students who have never gone through divorce, those by students who have been divorced, and those by students whose parents have been divorced. Do the essays differ because of this difference in experience? You may want to share the results with the class.

2. One way for students to effectively write on a crisis is to consider the differences that might exist between a family disrupted by divorce, fire, death, job loss, or relocation. This may help students focus on the attributes of family life that are affected by their crisis.

What Are Friends?

ON FRIENDSHIP

Margaret Mead and Rhoda Metraux

<u>Questions for Study and Discussion (p. 182)</u>

1. In paragraph 4, Mead and Metraux describe Americans' conception of the term "friend": "[It] can be applied to a wide range of relationships--to someone one has known for a few weeks in a new place, to a close business associate, to a childhood playmate, to a man or a woman, to a trusted confidant. There are real differences among these relations for Americans--a friendship may be superficial, casual, situational or deep and enduring." Europeans, though, do not see the differences in these relations and, according to Mead and Metraux, believe that "people known and accepted temporarily, casually, flow in and out of Americans' homes with little ceremony and often with little personal commitment" (5).

Students' reactions to Mead and Metraux's definition may vary. Those who have traveled abroad may have insights to share in regard to how Europeans view friendship both for themselves and for Americans.

2. The authors' purpose is to explain. This is evident by the statement presented in paragraph 6--"Who, then, is a friend?" which is repeated in slightly different form in the concluding paragraph--"What, then, is friendship?" Mead and Metraux attempt to arrive at an internationally applicable definition of friendship.

3. According to Mead and Metraux, in France "friendship is a one-to-one relationship that demands a keen awareness of the other person's intellect, temperament and particular interests. A friend is someone who draws out your own best qualities" (9). French friendships are also compartmentalized--"Different friends fill different niches in each person's life" (10). In Germany, "friendship is much more articulately a matter of feeling" and "friendships are based on mutuality of feeling" (13), in contrast to the French inclination toward intellectuality and lively disagreement. Finally, in England the basis for friendship is "shared activity" and usually takes place outside the family (14).

Students' responses to these types of friendship may vary. Some may note how American views on friendship tend to incorporate aspects of all three of the above.

4. Mead and Metraux see the difference between friendship and kinship as being the necessity of invoking a freedom of choice--"A friend is someone who chooses and is chosen" (15), whereas kinship is a matter of blood relations.

5. In the last sentence of their essay Mead and

Metraux state that "the American's characteristic openness to different styles of relationship makes it possible for him to find new friends abroad with whom he feels at home."

Writing Topics (p. 183)

1. In responding to these three questions students will likely incorporate elements of definition, illustration, and process analysis into their essays. It may therefore be helpful to review these patterns of organization and development before they begin. You can also review samples of each as they appear in the other essays on friendship in this section.

2. For different perspectives on the nature of relationships between men and women, you can have students review Marc Feigen Fasteau's "Friendships among Men" (p. 189), Judith Viorst's "Friends, Good Friends--and Such Good Friends" (p. 184), and Susan Jacoby's "Unfair Game" (p. 207). You can also discuss how the possibility of friendship between men and women is affected by how the issue of women's rights is perceived by those involved.

FRIENDS, GOOD FRIENDS--AND SUCH GOOD FRIENDS

Judith Viorst

Questions for Study and Discussion (p. 188)

1. Friends, Viorst once would have said, "totally love, support, and trust each other, and bare to each other the secrets of their soul, and run--no questions asked--to help each other, and tell harsh truths to each other" (1). In short, she once would have maintained that "a friend is a friend all the way" (3). But as a result of the friendships she has had and observed over the years, she now believes that this view is a "narrow" one.

2. Viorst is attempting to demonstrate that friendships "are conducted at many levels of intensity, serve many different functions, meet different needs and range from the intense friendship of soul sisters mentioned above to that of the most nonchalant and casual playmates" (3). Her categories support this thesis by illustrating the diversity of friendship.

3. Had she been writing for an audience of young men, Viorst's essay would have included the categories of business friends and female friends, and possibly also of drinking friends. For the feminine examples, she would have substituted masculine examples such as friends who talk sports (under "special interest" friends), fraternity "brothers" ("crossroads friends"), and so on.

4. Viorst uses quotations to supplement her own experience, for example in paragraphs 26 and 27 where she includes Lucy's comments on friendship with a man. These

additions provide additional support for her thesis, and are
therefore appropriate. They are, however, rather pat--as if
Viorst had gone around interviewing her woman friends on the
subject of friendship, or as if she had invented some or all
of the quotations herself.

    5. By using the pronoun "we," Viorst establishes a
personal relationship with her reader, as though she were
engaging in a heart-to-heart talk with a woman friend. The
technique is successful where the reader agrees with and
identifies with Viorst but may prove annoying where the
reader's experiences do not match Viorst's--as some student
readers may point out.

    6. The tone of the essay is intimate and occasionally
wryly humorous. See, for example, paragraph 1 ("no, you
can't wear that dress unless you lose ten pounds first"),
the phrase "maybe some mommy with whom we serve juice and
cookies each week at the Glenwood Co-op Nursery" (5), paragraph 13, ("But since [oh shame!] I care a lot about eye-
shadows, hemlines, and shoes. . . ."), and the humorous
climactic revelations of the final paragraph.

Writing Topics (p. 188)

    1. This question is intended to give students experi-
ence writing an extended definition. To a considerable
degree that definition will be personal or indeed
arbitrary--on what grounds can one prove Viorst's viewpoint
right or wrong? So the object of the students' exploration
should be to arrive at a clear and coherent statement and to
illustrate it in a reasonable and engaging way.

    2. In responding to this question students might begin
by deciding which position they wish to emphasize (the
advantages or the disadvantages of American familiarity),
and by constructing an appropriate thesis statement with
which to organize the essay. For example, one student might
argue that while American informality may make social and
professional exchanges easier, it also blurs the distinction
between acquaintances and real friends.

FRIENDSHIPS AMONG MEN

Marc Feigen Fasteau

Questions for Study and Discussion (p. 197)

    1. As Fasteau explains in paragraph 2, the belief that
the great friendships are between men is a myth because
usually "something is missing. Despite the time men spend
together, their contact rarely goes beyond the external, a
limitation which tends to make their friendships shallow and
unsatisfying."

    2. See #1 above.

    3. In paragraph 12 Fasteau states: "The sources of

this stifling ban on self-disclosure, the reasons why men hide from each other, lie in the taboos and imperatives of the masculine stereotype." These taboos and imperatives include the belief that men are supposed to be functional, the obsessive competitiveness that often exists between male friends, and the fear of being or being thought homosexual.

Men rationalize this fear of intimacy, according to Fasteau, by convincing themselves that only those men whose problems have overwhelmed them, in other words, only weak men, feel the need for self-disclosure and expressiveness.

4. Fasteau believes that games play such an important role in men's lives because they "stave off a lull in which they would be together without some impersonal focus for their attention" (5). Games give men something besides themselves to talk about.

Women also use games as a means for getting together, but "the games themselves are not the only means of communication" (5-note).

5. The exceptions that Fasteau notes when men will become personal are: 1) when they are drunk; 2) when they are talking to strangers; and 3) when they are in a mixed group and can depend on women to facilitate the conversation.

6. Fasteau believes that "competitiveness feeds the most basic obstacle to openness between men, the inability to admit to being vulnerable" (17).

Students' responses to this belief may vary and it may be interesting to note if there are significant differences between male and female responses.

7. This last question can facilitate an open-ended discussion in which you analyze the way male friends are currently portrayed in the media. You can also ask students to consider the cause and effect relationship of this portrayal. Do the media simply reflect attitudes as they already exist? or do they help establish and foster the way men look at each other as friends?

Writing Topics (p. 197)

1. Students may find it helpful to take one aspect of Fasteau's analysis of male friendships and use it as the basis for a refutation. For instance, some may find that his conclusions about the role games play in male relationships do not allow for the positive effects that games can contribute. An argumentative counteranalysis of games could then demonstrate how such contact does, at times, go beyond the "external."

2. A prewriting discussion, in which you generate ideas about why men "hide from each other" and how they might communicate more meaningfully, may help students get started on this assignment. One way to approach such a discussion is to consider ways that women differ from men in

their ability to communicate with each other, and to speculate on whether these differences could ever be incorporated
in male views on friendship.

MY FRIEND, ALBERT EINSTEIN

Banesh Hoffmann

Questions for Study and Discussion (p. 202)

1. According to Hoffmann, Einstein was unpretentious
in appearance, uninterested in salary, utterly natural,
gentle, deeply religious, practical, and unassuming.

2. No doubt Hoffmann wanted to de-mystify Einstein, to
show that behind the great mind was a warm, real human
being. In paragraph 24 Hoffmann states directly that his
purpose is to explain to the reader what it was like to work
with Einstein.

3. The anecdotes _show_ us what Einstein was like, and
so are far preferable to general statements about Einstein.
Some of these anecdotes are Einstein's covering of his hat
in the rain and Hoffmann's first meeting with Einstein. The
anecdotes demonstrate Einstein's "simplicity," both in terms
of his logical mind and his self-deprecating, down-to-earth
nature.

4. Rather than present a strictly chronological account of Einstein's life, one that many readers might find
uninteresting, Hoffmann begins with the surprising statement, "He was one of the greatest scientists the world has
ever known, yet if I had to convey the essence of Albert
Einstein in a single word, I would choose _simplicity_."

5. Einstein had a "knack for going instinctively to
the heart of a matter." According to Hoffmann, Einstein,
like Mozart, could discover what "had always existed as part
of the inner beauty of the Universe, waiting to be revealed." For that reason, the answers often seemed so
simple that Hoffmann could have "kicked" himself for not
having thought them.

6. The two theories were seemingly contradictory. For
one man to propose both as correct simultaneously was revo-
lutionary and controversial, and demonstrated his brilliance.

7. The walk on the beach is reminiscent of an earlier
scene in the essay. It is particularly poignant because it
reminds the reader that the loveliest scenes hold within
them the infinite wisdom of the universe. That the scene
holds a "sadder" beauty may be a reference to the destructive powers of the atom, unleashed as a result of Einstein's
quest for "cosmic simplicity."

Writing Topics (p. 202)

1. In order to facilitate this assignment, you may make available examples of the writings of the Greek philosophers, such as Socrates, Plato, and Aristotle, or the ideas of math greats such as Archimedes and Euclid, and inventors such as Eli Whitney, Benjamin Franklin, and Thomas Edison. Students can discover for themselves what similarities seem to arise among those we designate as geniuses.

2. Before students begin work on this assignment, you may wish to review with them the practice of supporting general or abstract statements with specific and concrete information. Since they are dealing with abstract concepts their essays should include very specific and concrete representations of how they feel about the person they are describing.

3 / MEN AND WOMEN

Gender Roles

UNFAIR GAME

Susan Jacoby

Questions for Study and Discussion (p. 210)

1. Susan Jacoby's thesis is stated in paragraph 6: "In Holiday Inns and at the Plaza, on buses and airplanes, in tourist and first class, a woman is always thought to be looking for a man in addition to whatever else she may be doing." Her article demonstrates how untrue that stereotype is, and was evidently written both to encourage women to assert themselves and to instruct men in common courtesy.

2. Jacoby advocates rebuffing the man with a polite but firm refusal and, should that fail, by telling him "roughly and loudly" that his presence is a "nuisance" (17).

3. In paragraph 17 Jacoby explains, "Our mothers didn't teach us to tell a man to get lost; they told us to smile and hint that we'd be just delighted to spend time with the gentleman if we didn't have other commitments." Evidently she herself is not constrained by that code.

4. She manages to imply that had she not been in a hurry, she might have stayed over in Dallas with him--which is not true, but which he will later have to explain to his wife.

5. Jacoby's essay is written in an assertive, straight-to-the-point manner. Her forthright "I do blame a man for trying in this situation" (15) and her crisp sentence fragments, "simple courtesy. No insults and hurt feelings" (19), are examples of that tone.

1. Women might be expected to have appreciated Jacoby's argument, and they did. The men, however, were less appreciative; many assumed that any woman without an escort in a bar or restaurant does intend to be picked up, or that the exceptions are so rare that such an assumption is natural and excusable. In preparation for writing their opinion letters, students may find it useful to read some "Letters to the Editor" in the New York Times (or the local newspaper) and discuss which are effective and which illogical or otherwise unpersuasive.

2. As always, it's the examples on which the effectiveness of the students' papers will depend. They might be encouraged to prepare for this assignment by considering a wide range of situations--at home, in class, at work, with friends, or just on the bus--and imagining the likely effects of courtesy and discourtesy.

3. An interesting approach to this question is to have students compare articles on dating from a contemporary issue of a magazine such as Seventeen and an early 1980's issue of that magazine, using back issues or microfilm in the library. Your male and female students will likely have very different answers to the last part of the question-- probably to their surprise.

LET 'EM EAT LEFTOVERS

Mike McGrady

Questions for Study and Discussion (p. 214)

1. The "happy housewife" is a mythical creature promulgated by the "Total Woman" or "Fascinating Womanhood people." McGrady approaches the image and its adherents with good-humored skepticism.

2. Housecleaning is ultimately futile--six hours work can be undone in six minutes. Central to McGrady's dissatisfaction is the tediousness of most housekeeping chores, as well as the bad pay and long hours.
He doesn't feel guilty about being a bad homemaker because he sees the role as mindless and unfulfilling, and thus nothing to take pride in.

3. Parenting is the "one solid reward" McGrady sees in being a homemaker: the opportunity to spend time caring for and enjoying one's children.

4. McGrady suggests that some women are afraid of the challenges of the outside world. But he encourages those already in rebellion "to stop pampering the rest of the family--let 'em eat leftovers" (15). His point is that women shouldn't feel guilty about a little benign neglect.

5. A new title would do nothing to alleviate the monotony and mindlessness of housework.

6. McGrady's audience is the general middle-class public, readers of <u>Newsweek</u>, both men and women. Although his advice is primarily for those women already in rebellion against the mindlessness of housework, McGrady's method of development is particularly persuasive because in describing the negative aspects of the job, he is appealing to a male perspective.

7. McGrady's title encourages self-preservation. In his view, those who might see it as callous reveal a lack of understanding almost as selfish as Marie Antoinette's.

8. Examples of sarcasm include the description of the "happy housewife" in paragraph 2, the list of jobs in paragraph 4, the image of the elevator operator in paragraph 6, the new titles suggested in paragraph 7, and the comparison of husbands to plantation owners in paragraph 12.

The effect is to deflate the sentimental image of the perfect homemaker.

9. The headings here are like humorous signposts, directing attention to McGrady's main points of discussion.

Writing Topics (p. 214)

1. It may be helpful to review with students the elements of effective argumentation, including the two basic types of presentation--logical and persuasive; the use of INDUCTIVE or DEDUCTIVE REASONING; and the avoidance of LOGICAL FALLACIES. For further explanations of these you can review the entry for each in the Glossary.

2. For this assignment some students will probably have experiences to offer where both parents are working and taking care of household chores together. As a prewriting activity, therefore, you can discuss with them some of the effects of living in a household where both parents work. Your discussion should yield examples of how the traditional roles are giving way to varied and interesting arrangements in many marriages. You might also ask students whether these arrangements have placed any more responsibility on them compared to students whose households have one parent who stays home.

THE ANDROGYNOUS MAN

Noel Perrin

Questions for Study and Discussion (p. 218)

1. In paragraph 7, Perrin states that "to be spiritually androgynous is a kind of freedom" which allows "a range of choices" not available, for example, to men who feel they have to imitate the stereotype of the "all-male, or he-man, or 100% red-blooded Americans."

Before revealing this definition Perrin felt it necessary to provide an example of how men are expected to fulfill certain roles and assume certain attitudes. This example serves as an effective introduction to the central issue of the essay--androgynes.

Perrin does not, however, use the strict dictionary sense of "androgyny," which involves the physical combination of a man and a woman in one body. Instead, he clearly refers to a "spiritual androgyny" that incorporates the attitudes and behaviors of both stereotyped sexual roles into a lifestyle that offers a wider range of choices.

2. A thesis for this essay might read as follows: "Androgynous men and women live freer lives than those who struggle to fit themselves into stereotyped masculine and feminine roles."

Perrin's purpose is to convince readers not to feel obliged to live up to prescribed roles as a condition for their own self-esteem, especially since androgynes are spiritually freer and live richer lives than those who try to be what they feel they have to be.

3. Perrin believes that androgynes have a wider range of choices in their lives are therefore freer than those who feel compelled to imitate rigid gender stereotypes. To support this belief he provides a series of examples from his own experiences: being freed to serve as a nurturing mother to his children; feeling free to kiss his cat; being unembarrassed about his ignorance of cars and household maintenance; and being more easily moved to public displays of emotion.

Students may find a couple of these examples less convincing than the others and, after discussing with them which these might be, see if they can assess why Perrin has chosen the particular examples he has included.

4. Though the essay can certainly appeal to both sexes, especially since its central issue is androgyny, its focus on the qualities of the "he-man" and its selection of examples geared toward male behavior suggest that its primary audience is men.

5. The point of Perrin's last paragraph is that men should feel free to act unself-consciously, regardless of the types of behavior such freedom might elicit. The public display of emotion is effective in conveying this because it is a classic example of the kind of behavior the stereotyped male would struggle to repress. Perrin suggests that not repressing such behavior is not a weakness but a kind of fulfillment.

Writing Topics (p. 218)

1. For a consideration of the pressure exerted on females to live up to certain sexual roles, students can review Susan Jacoby's "Unfair Game" and Mike McGrady's "Let 'Em Eat Leftovers." After looking over their discussions of what is expected of women and men, and at Perrin's discussion of the "he-man," students may find it easier to identify how their own definitions of masculinity and femininity

differ from prevailing stereotypes. Students may profit from a class discussion of how their own views of sexual roles differ from those of their parents.

2. Some students may find it helpful to approach this assignment from the opposite direction, recounting experiences where they were forced to recognize that formerly accepted stereotyped roles were, in fact, no longer valid. They can then discuss what effect this recognition has had on their views toward other prescribed roles for men and women.

SHILOH

Bobbie Ann Mason

<u>Questions for Study and Discussion (p. 230)</u>

1. While Leroy was away form home, Norma Jean could live the way she wanted and Leroy did not get in the way. Now he is ever-present. Norma Jean wants to better herself and her life and she thinks this is not possible in a relationship with Leroy. Her discontent is not a direct result of the accident. However, dealing with Leroy--all day, everyday--disallowed any dilution of their problems.

2. The diction of the characters indicates they come from the working class. They work at blue collar jobs. The presents they buy and the crafts that Leroy is interested in are meant to be stereotypical of working-class tastes, as are the meals Norma Jean prepares.

3. In the beginning of the story, Norma Jean accepts Leroy and what he has to say. However, as the story moves along, Norma Jean shows less interest and increasing annoyance in what Leroy has to say. In paragraph 43, Norma Jean reveals that she has looked into possible jobs for Leroy to get him out and earning some money. After that Leroy realizes that during his absences Norma Jean has become someone he doesn't know and that he has become someone she doesn't like. Norma Jean's resistance to Leroy's dream of the log cabin symbolizes this growing distance between them and leads to her intention to leave him.

4. Mabel is not superfluous; she is the window through which Leroy realizes he does not really know Norma Jean or what her life was like while he was out working.

5. The battlefield symbolizes not only a beginning for the victors, but an end for the defeated. As such, the battlefield was the beginning of Mabel's marriage and the end of Norma Jean's. Therefore, it is not surprising, but fitting that Norma Jean chose the battlefield to tell Leroy her intentions. Because it has such opposite meanings for Mabel and Norma Jean, the reader sees that the mother and daughter are very different people, which explains why their relationship is sometimes rocky.

6. Although she may not be aware of it, Norma Jean has

become a feminist, in that she is finally looking at her life, establishing her own identity and deciding she is ready to "grow." To do that she is taking body-building and writing classes, experimenting with new hobbies such as cooking and playing the organ. Leroy's befuddlement over Norma Jean's changed behavior contrasts with Norma Jean's certainty about what she wants.

7. Norma Jean is waving her arms, victoriously, in an expression of freedom.

Writing Topics (p. 231)

1. Before students begin this assignment, it may be helpful to review with them the two approaches for organizing information in a comparison and/or contrast--the block method, where they would discuss all the characteristics of each woman and them compare and/or contrast them to all the features of the other; and the point-by point method, where they would compare and/or contrast the individual aspects of each woman side by side. Remind students to analyze their information carefully to see which of these approaches would be best suited for their purpose.

2. For this assignment it may be necessary for students to do some extra reading about the philosophies of the feminist movement and take into consideration who the author is in regard to background, wealth, education, and job. If the student is able to find a variety of authors, the tone may convey different attitudes and concerns of the movement. This may be an interesting topic of discussion as the feminist writings of Kate Chopin may differ greatly from feminists of today.

Men and Women in the Workplace

THE IMPORTANCE OF WORK

Gloria Steinem

Questions for Study and Discussion (p. 237)

1. Students' responses should reflect Steinem's main concern--that women be allowed to work not just because they feel they have to, but because "productive, honored work [is] a natural part of ourselves and . . . one of life's basic pleasures" (22).

2. Many women greeted the Wall Street Journal's definition of "the working woman" with cynicism because women have always worked, if not in the salaried labor force, in the "poorly rewarded, low-security, high-risk job of home-making" (2). Steinem's response to the Journal's definition is the following: "If all the productive work of human maintenance that women do in the home were valued at its

replacement cost, the gross national product of the United States would go up by 26 percent (2).

3. Steinem believes many women use this response to ward off criticism that they are not taking care of their children, or that they are unfeminine, or to confront men's resentment of them competing in the work force. The strongest objections Steinem has to this "Womenworkbecause-wehaveto" defense are that it ignores the rewards of work that women who use it are not confessing, and it can lead to considerable waste of human talents.

Steinem explains the significance of turning this phrase into a single word in paragraph 7: "The phrase has become one word, one key on the typewriter--an economic form of the socially 'feminine' stance of passivity and self-sacrifice. Under attack, we still tend to present ourselves as creatures of economic necessity and familial devotion. 'Womenworkbecausewehaveto' has become the easiest thing to say."

4. Steinem dismisses these claims by simply stating "that a decent job is a basic human right for everybody" (6).

5. Steinem applauds women who work even though they don't need to financially because they "are on the frontier of asserting this right for all women. . . . to prevent a woman whose husband or father is wealthy from earning her own living, and from gaining the self-confidence that comes with that ability, is to keep her needful of that unearned power and less willing to dispense it. Moreover, it is to lose forever her unique talents" (18).

6. In the Economic Recovery Act of 1946 "full employ-ment" was reinterpreted and defined as "the employment of those who want to work, without regard to whether their employment is, by some definition, necessary." Steinem strongly supports this definition and recognizes its impor-tance especially in bad economic times, since bad times often create a "resentment of employed women" (13).

7. According to Steinem, society benefits from full employment of men and women because it needs "all its mem-bers' talents" (12). Benefits to individuals are anchored on the notion that men and women both "are more satisfied with their lives" when they hold jobs by choice.

8. Steinem's article is firmly but calmly expressed and her main points well-reasoned, making her effective as a persuasive writer. She does not use a tone or diction that is openly hostile to women who may rely on the "wework-becausewehaveto" defense, and thereby ingratiates herself with those readers who are most important to her purpose. Her explanations are logical and clearly reasoned, and the supporting information suited to the needs of her main idea.

9. This article seems intended mainly for women, par-ticularly those who may rely on a "Womenworkbecausewehaveto" defense of their jobs. Steinem assumes that most of her readers will recognize that the points she raises about the

value of holding a job are, for the most part, taken for granted with respect to men, and only come into question when they are applied to women. Her argument may therefore be more convincing for those who sympathize with that central premise than for those who would question the need for such an application in the first place, thereby obscuring their appreciation of her argument that women should openly recognize the value and rewards of the jobs they hold.

Writing Topics (p. 238)

1. A prewriting discussion for this topic may generate some lively debate on the issue of two-income families and society's obligation to protect the right of <u>both</u> parents to work. An analysis of this issue within the context of the position stated in the assignment may help students arrive at some conclusions about the pros and cons of attempting to provide a job for <u>every</u> citizen.
2. Students may find it enlightening to share the results of this assignment and discover some of the effects that different parents' working situations have on their children's lives.

SUMMER JOB

Mary Mebane

Questions for Study and Discussion (p. 244)

1. Mebane knew the work would be hard because several women in her neighborhood had already worked at American during the green season and had informed her that mostly whites worked on the "cigarette side" where the work was easy; she would, instead, work the belt on the "tobacco side" where it would be more difficult.
Had the section on the hiring process been shortened, Mebane's essay would be less effective. The monotony and aggravation the women endure while standing on line all day in oppressive heat, just to get jobs of such miserable circumstances, indicate how much they need the work and money these temporary jobs offered, and emphasize the discriminatory and exploitative practices of the tobacco company.
2. Mebane worked on two different belts once she was hired. On the first, she sifted through shredded tobacco and picked out pieces whose stems were too large. After only a short while there, she moved upstairs to "work up" bundles of tobacco on to another belt, making sure the tied ends faced her before the bundles went off to the cutter. At the end of her first day of such work, bending over barrels of tied tobacco leaves, then over the belt, and then back over the barrels, Mebane says she "found the work killing" (23).

60

3. So many women sought work at the tobacco factories because they could make "their chief money of the year" during the green season, as "the factory paid more money than days work" (1).

Since this work was temporary, though, it likely meant that most men could not afford to leave whatever permanent jobs they had, thereby making the work available to women instead.

4. Mebane uses contrast mainly to show the different conditions for African-Americans and whites. Before she even goes for the job, she realizes that the easy work on the cigarette side is mostly for whites and the "killing work" of the belts on the tobacco side for African-Americans. While waiting to be chosen for work, the mass of African-American women are left standing in the sweltering sun while the white men doing the hiring are in the relative comfort of the air-conditioned office. And when the pudgy man occasionally appears to call the women to work his manner is casual, indifferent, and nonchalant, in contrast to the pushing and shoving of the women as they struggle to be noticed and chosen for a job. This series of contrasts points up the injustice Mebane feels as she looks back on her experiences with the American Tobacco Company.

5. Mebane stayed on at her job only because her neighbors "were quite pleased that [she] had gotten on" and she did not "want to let them down" by quitting.

6. Students may cite instances of Mebane's use of detail from almost any section of the essay, but will probably focus most particularly on the two days she waits to be chosen and on each of the belts she works after she is hired. They should recognize that such detail helps convey a more accurate and concrete sense of what Mebane's experiences were like, making the underlying sense of racial injustice more strongly felt.

7. Mebane identifies the time, place, and circumstances of her narrative in the first two paragraphs. Her first sentence establishes the time as the summer of 1949. From there she explains the "green season" and that there were two tobacco companies in Durham, only one of which—American—hired temporary workers, thereby providing the place. In paragraph two, she reveals the rest of the circumstances needed to appreciate the beginning of the narrative proper, which begins with paragraph three.

Writing Topics (p. 245)

1. This topic provides a good opportunity to review elements of process analysis. Students will be concerned with "directional process" and can find a definition for that term in the glossary. In addition, you may wish to work through a model directional process essay with them, outlining the stages of a proposed essay according to how the steps in a selected process fall into place.

2. Since many students may not have any direct experi-

ence with full-time year-round employment, they may wish to
approach this topic by considering how their attitude toward
the summer jobs they've held was affected by knowing they
would be finished working when the summer ended. How might
they have felt if there were no such end in sight? By
considering this idea, students may be better able to speculate on the differences and similarities that exist between
summer and full-time work.

NURSES

Lewis Thomas

Questions for Study and Discussion (p. 250)

1. Thomas's thesis is stated in the last paragraph and
is most effective there, since to present it any earlier
may lead readers to dismiss as exorbitant his support for
nurses.
2. The major difference between Thomas's description
of nursing in his mother's day and nursing today is that the
dominant concern or duty for his mother was always the care
of patients, whereas today nurses are being asked to "take
on more and more purely administrative tasks" (5). He
accounts for this change by explaining that nurses now must
oversee staffs of LPN's, ward maids, porters, and other
workers who perform duties that used to be part of a nurse's
obligation.
3. Thomas's comparison and contrast of his mother's
nursing duties to those of nurses today emphasizes the
continuing sense of hard work and immense value associated
with their roles, while at the same time revealing the
changes that have occurred and what those changes have meant
in terms of patient care.
4. In paragraph 5 Lewis states: "Too late maybe, the
nurses have begun to realize that they are gradually being
excluded from the one duty which had previously been their
most important reward but which had been so taken for granted that nobody mentioned it in listing the duties of a
nurse: close personal contact with patients."
5. As Thomas states it, "nursing education has been
upgraded in recent years." Hospital schools that used to
provide high school graduates with an RN certificate after
two or three years "have been replaced by schools attached
to colleges and universities, with a four-year curriculum
leading simultaneously to a bachelor's degree and an RN
certificate" (5). This has, in turn, led to more of a
"standoffish, often adversarial relationship between nurses
and doctors," as doctors "worry that nurses are trying to
move away from their historical responsibilities to medicine
. . . [and] nurses assert that they are their own profession
. . . coequal colleagues with physicians" (6).
6. Thomas describes, in paragraph 8, "the constant

interplay [in hospitals] of powerful forces pulling away at each other in different directions." These forces include interns, attending physicians, diagnostic laboratories, medical students, administrators, and "each individual worker in the place." His conclusion, then, "is that the institution is held together, GLUED together, enabled to function as an organism, by the nurses and by nobody else" (9).

Thomas's understanding of the vital role nurses perform for hospitals is the result of firsthand observations, "having been an apprehensive patient [himself] off and on over a three-year period on the wards of the hospital for which [he worked]" (7).

7. It appears obvious that Thomas's father's "deep and lasting respect for the whole nursing profession" has rubbed off on his son, and that that respect was due in large part to the work of Thomas's mother.

Writing Topics (p. 250)

1. This topic provides a good opportunity to use debate as a prewriting activity. To lead such a debate you can elicit responses both for and against the proposition presented, and then explore with students the validity and ramifications for each. Your discussion may give students a more comprehensive informational context from which to consider this assignment.

2. Since Thomas's essay deals with nursing, you may wish to discuss the difficulties encountered by males in that profession as a prewriting activity for this topic. Consider the issue from the perspectives of the male nurse himself, his female coworkers, hospital administrators, doctors, patients, and the male nurse's friends and family members. By examining this particular area in depth, students may be better able to consider ideas and draw conclusions about the difficulties encountered in other professions by those who confront fellow-workers predominantly of the opposite sex.

CONFESSIONS OF A WORKING STIFF

Patrick Fenton

Questions for Study and Discussion (p. 256)

1. Fenton feels that Seaboard World Airlines is insensitive to his needs as a human being.

He feels his job is very difficult and does not allow him to use his mind at all.

The immediate causes of his dissatisfaction are the "drudgery, boredom, and fatigue" (1) of his job.

Fenton continues to work for the airline because he wants to provide for his children and pay the mortgage. The job has dampened his enthusiasm and initiative, and he therefore does not try to get another job.

2. The company, in our view, seems to be more interested in automation than in improving working conditions. The company's basic motive is profit, and it will improve working conditions if, and only if, profits are improved. There was apparently little likelihood of doing this at Seaboard.

We feel that the airline company gets nervous because an employee is stepping out of line--thinking is not regarded as part of his job.

3. The "leads," as Fenton tells us, are "foremen who must keep the men moving" (16). Fenton feels that it is important to discuss them because they are a prime example of employees who once had pride in their jobs and who now have only apathy.

4. Diction and imagery which suggest the regimented, prisonlike existence of the men are found in paragraphs 11, 12, 15, and 16.

5. Paragraphs 5, 8, 18, and 30 rely heavily on concrete details. Incidents which dramatize the plight of the workers occur in paragraphs 13, 14, and 21 through 25.

In each case Fenton _shows_ rather than _tells_ us about the plight of the workers.

6. We feel that each of these similes is appropriate in its context.

7. Fenton means that he is a working corpse, that his job has taken the life out of him.

8. According to Fenton, "It's not the hard work that breaks a man at the airline, it's the boredom of doing the same job over and over again" (19).

Writing Topics (p. 257)

1. Students may wish to focus on how the degree to which a job requires one to think is related to the satisfaction that can be derived from work. Students can also consider the traditional conception of blue-collar versus white-collar, and evaluate the role that productive thought plays in our regard for each.

2. If students wish to do some research into the current state of relations between management and labor they can seek out any of the numerous recent publications that examine the role and quality of business in our lives. Two of the more prominent examples of such pop analyses are: Megatrends: Ten New Directions Transforming Our Lives by John Naisbitt; and In Search of Excellence by Thomas J. Peters and Robert H. Waterman, Jr.

WHY MARRIED MOTHERS WORK

Victor Fuchs

Questions for Study and Discussion (p. 262)

1. The rise in wages and the expansion of the service sector have led to an increase of women and mothers in the work force. Fuchs provides ample evidence to support his thesis, leaving the reader little room for disagreement. Because he dispels several formerly held myths about why mothers work, the reader will find it difficult to add to his list of reasons.

2. Fuchs uses statistics from the Employment and Training Administration, as well as quotes and book excerpts. The quotes may not be all that convincing to some students, because Fuchs does not explain who the experts are or what books he drew from. The reader should be more impressed with Fuchs's interpretation of statistics as they relate to his thesis.

3. Fuchs relies on logical appeal by listing statistics and percentages to explain the growth of mothers in the work force as it relates to other occurrences. See paragraphs 3-8 in which he interprets data and translates it into percentages.

4. The married mother is traditionally last in terms of economic need or available time for a job. More and more the women who work are those who must work to support themselves. Married mothers have long been thought to stay home with the children while the husband works. Fuchs's thesis is completely stated in paragraph 8. In the first seven paragraphs he argues against long-held beliefs so that by time he states his thesis at the end of the essay, it is already well-supported.

5. Fuchs supports this argument well, even though he has two people claiming the opposite. His point, that you cannot explain a variable with a constant, is reasonable. The way in which he supports his thesis forces the reader to consider the possibility that we cannot turn alone to the solitary subjects of a study to find out "why?" We must look at the issue as a whole, over a period of time.

6. The topic sentence is the first sentence of each paragraph. By beginning thus, Fuchs achieves a classification of the "causes" for mothers working.

7. In paragraph 6, Fuchs discusses the difference between the "cause" of an occurrence and the response to it. It seems that Fuchs himself may have confused response and cause in his discussion of the increase in time-saving devices. The reader will assume that having these innovations made it easier for mothers to go to work. However, Fuchs theorizes that it is women's increased working outside the home that made these innovations necessary. Fuchs does not firmly argue this point with statistics or dates. The

reader can say that he has confused the cause with the response, or that he has not argued his side well.

8. Fuchs begins by stating that married mothers are entering the work force at increased rates. In the next five paragraphs he explains that the increase is not due to the feminist movement, government affirmative action programs, or because it is "needed." He then explains the dangers of confusing the cause with the response while explaining that the increase is not because the time saving innovations have made it easier for women to get jobs. In paragraphs 8 through 10 Fuchs argues that the increase is because of the higher wages available and the growth of the service sector. He concludes by theorizing what effects the increase in the female work force will have on society. This structure is effective because it dispels formerly held beliefs, making the reader more susceptible to Fuchs's thesis. The reader is also more likely to remember Fuchs's thesis since it is stated at the end of the essay.

Writing Topics (p. 262)

1. Many of the students in class will have or be working mothers and can shed light on this subject. During class you may want to graph the typical week for a working mother to see if a forty-hour week is feasible. You may want the students to consider whether it is feasible for the company they work for.

2. You may even discuss this topic with your colleagues to get other opinions. After discussing the changes you can report the various answers to your students. It may also be interesting for you to discuss your experiences as a student so students have a reference from a student's view of college in the past. They can then determine the differences the students' lives have gone through from your college days and theirs and evaluate the political, environmental, and educational priorities.

4 / CAMPUS LIFE

The Aims of Education

A NATION AT RISK

David P. Gardner

Questions for Study and Discussion (p. 274)

1. The main point of the commission's report is stated at the beginning and at the end of this selection--America is at risk because of the decline in its overall educational achievements, and it is necessary to act now to renew our commitment to educational excellence. The basic assumption

underlying this argument is that "American prosperity, security, and civility" depend on the education of its inhabitants, and that a "rising tide of mediocrity . . . [at] . . . the educational foundations of our society . . . threatens our very future as a Nation and a people" (11).

Students' responses to this evaluation of the role and condition of education in our society may vary.

2. In paragraph 3 Gardner writes: "This report . . . seeks to generate reform of our educational system in fundamental ways to renew the Nation's commitment to schools and colleges of high quality throughout the length and breadth of our land."

3. Gardner's reference to a "rising tide of mediocrity" is simply a figurative way to describe the increasing level of unacceptable performance in our Nation's schools, and suggests that unless we do something to prevent it this tide will become a wave that crashes over us in the form of America's preeminence in the world being displaced.

The "Sputnik challenge" refers to the sharp increase in both commitment and performance in areas of education, particularly in the sciences, as a response to the Soviet Union accomplishing the first successful space launch.

And the "information age" is the label that has been attached to the shift from an economy based on industrial consumerism, represented most significantly by the central role of automobile manufacturing, to an economy based on the creation and exchange of information facilitated by ever-expanding means of electronic communication.

4. Students' responses will obviously vary according to their experiences in high school. This question can therefore serve as a good focus for class discussion.

5. Aside from a few references to the standard measuring device for student performance--SAT scores--there is little concrete evidence to document the claims presented in "Indicators of the Risk." Instead, Gardner relies on such phrases as "International comparisons of student achievement," "Average achievement . . . on most standardized tests," "tested ability with comparable achievement in school," "the 'higher order' skills we should expect of them," and "Business and military leaders complain," as well as on figures and percentages that do not reveal how they were arrived at. Students' reactions to the vagueness of this documentation may vary.

6. Gardner reveals the characteristics of a Learning Society in paragraph 26: 1) the commitment to a set of values and to a system of education that affords all members the opportunity to stretch their minds to full capacity, from early childhood through adulthood, learning more as the world itself changes; 2) a basic foundation that education is important not only because of what it contributes to one's career goals but also because of the value it adds to the general quality of one's life; and 3) educational opportunities extending far beyond the traditional institutions of learning, our schools and colleges.

Students' opinions on whether the means to achieve such a Learning Society are already in place may vary. Some may believe the means are readily available but not in place so we need to commit ourselves to having those means serve their appropriate roles, while others may think the means are already in place and that we only require a renewed commitment to the purpose for which our educational systems were established.

7. The tone of the report is one of urgency. Words and phrases that contribute to this sense of urgency include the following:

risk; undergirds; eroded; rising tide of mediocrity; threatens (1)

act of war; squandered; unthinking; unilateral educational disarmament (2)

lost sight of (3)

compromised; conflicting demands; exact an educational cost (4)

History is not kind to idlers. (6)

indispensable investment (7)

effectively disenfranchised (8)

the progress of society itself (10)

risk (11)

chilling observations (13)

the problem does not stop there (14)

The negative impact . . . cannot be overstated (15)

tension between hope and frustration (16)

frustration threatens to overwhelm their hope (18)

dimming of personal expectations; fear of losing a shared vision (18)

This predicament (19)

undertone of frustration; significant political implications (20)

educationally encompassing need (21)

must be committed (22)

Our goal must be (24)

The task . . . is enormous and must be properly understood and taken seriously (25)

ever-accelerating; ever-greater; ever-larger (26)

vast mass shaped by tensions and pressures that inhibit
(27)

we issue this call; America is at risk (28)

8. Excellence is defined in paragraph 22. For the
individual learner "it means performing on the boundary of
individual ability in ways that test and push back personal
limits"; for schools and colleges it means setting "high
expectations and goals for all learners" and then trying "in
every way possible to help students reach them"; and for
society it means adopting "these policies, for it will then
be prepared through the education and skill of its people to
respond to the challenge of a rapidly changing world."
This definition is vital to understanding the report's
main thrust--that we need to combat the rising tide of
mediocrity in our schools through a renewed commitment to
excellence. The definition spells out exactly what that
means.

Writing Topics (p. 275)

1. Students should consider this topic in specific
relation to whether they think their own high schools set
"high expectations and goals for all learners." Most of
your students, by being in your class, were evidently successful in high school, yet a surprising number, if Gardner's report is correct, were rarely challenged to do their
best work. Have students examine whether this is the case
or not and, if so, where the fault might lie. This kind of
analysis may help them develop a focus for their essays.
2. As a prewriting activity you can discuss this topic
with students by comparing motivation for academic endeavors
to motivation in such areas as athletics or music or any
other extracurricular activity. By analyzing the relationship between motivation, challenge, and success in an area
of particular personal interest, students may be able to
draw conclusions, in comparison or contrast, about this
relationship as it applies to academic achievements.
3. One approach to this question is for each student
to consider how many of a typical day's activities and
transactions involve the use of computers. Some examples
include banking and credit cards; using the telephone;
driving a car (which was partly assembled by robots); listening to a record (if it was made using digital recording);

and shopping, as some stores have bar-code readers that automate their cash registers.

SOME VERY MODEST PROPOSALS FOR THE IMPROVEMENT OF AMERICAN EDUCATION

Nathan Glazer

Questions for Study and Discussion (p. 282)

1.   There are two possible definitions of "part-time." Professionals could come into the high school part-time and teach classes relative to their field. However, they could also share hours with a full-time teacher, allowing him or her to work less than forty hours. Having a professional from a business community teach Business Principals, for example, may be beneficial, as it will give students first-hand information. Obviously however, cutting into staff hours may alienate them and leave gaps in schedules.
2.   Glazer's last sentence sums up his call for "modest" but significant changes to the educational system. If we can make these simple changes, he argues, we can make a real difference in the classroom environment that may in turn create broader improvements.
3.   The more comfortable and happy a student is, the more easily he learns. Whether the environmental upgrades consist of simply removing distractions (i.e., removing windows in doors so students are not disturbed by others in the hall), or work to increase the individual student's esteem--anything done for the student's benefit will have some positive effects on the learning process.
4.   The "disarming" Glazer speaks of does not protect students, per se; instead it keeps them in line. Students may challenge Glazer's point that security guards around the country protect those who are coming in. They may point out that guards also keep track of those going out. Glazer seems to be blaming students who are bussed in for this problem, claiming that in the absence of security guards and locked doors, bussed students would cause enough trouble to make the schools unsafe. If this disarming would lead to bussed students, or anyone, causing more harm than they could before, this would be dangerous to the security of the school. However, it seems more likely that the major consequence will be that students will be able to leave the building unnoticed.
5.   Glazer seems to be describing inner-city school systems, those in Boston particularly. His example is not typical of a suburban school system. His reference to security problems and issues with minority students do not apply universally. If Glazer does not intend this description to be universally applied, he needs to be clearer about it.

6.   Glazer feels that the issuing of new editions of textbooks squanders efficiency. Teachers need to familiarize themselves with a given text and not be subject to constant changes. However, most texts do not change so drastically that teachers need to alter their course plan. Instead of "re-learning," teachers would need only take note of corrections, changes or additions. Although it is important to be familiar with a text, dedication to one book might result in stagnation and dependence on a single outline instead of a course and precious new information might be overlooked. For example, history students today need daily updates to keep track of changes in world politics.
7.   It would be hard to impose this on students. Many students do not have time outside of school hours for cleaning up. The alternative, to take part of the school day for cleanup, will reduce even further the time available for instruction.

Writing Topics (p. 282)

1.   Before students begin writing it may be helpful to review the section from the Introduction to this book on developing an argumentative essay, and to discuss in class the elements of a good argument. You can then go over Glazer's essay again and look closely at how it is constructed as an argument. Students may be able to use this information as a basis choosing the structure and organization of their own essays.
2.   This assignment may involve some research for the students. As a prewriting activity you may designate researchers of information on the schools and students involved. The students can share their research findings in class and discuss their reactions to the gathered information. The data collected and shared, as well as the ideas expressed in response to it, may help students formulate an approach for their essays.

TODAY'S UNIVERSITY--WHERE DEMOCRACY IS ANARCHY

Allan Bloom

Questions for Study and Discussion (p. 286)

1.   See the first paragraph where Bloom states that college is the "space between the intellectual wasteland . . . and the inevitable dreary professional training. . . . In this short time he must learn that there is a great world beyond the little one he knows." Many students will agree with this statement but may still disagree with Bloom's overall disregard for the need for a college education. Certainly it seems reasonable to argue that $40,000 is a high price to pay to become cultured. However, it can also be argued that there are certain vital intangibles a student

cannot learn through job training and apprenticeships--such as the value of an educated opinion, the knowledge of not only what can be learned, but how to go about it, and the craft of learning to think for oneself.

2. Bloom's overall tone in this essay is hostile. When referring to universities, he is sarcastic, using negatively charged words such as: <u>anarchy</u> and <u>imperial</u>. When speaking of the professional life, he sounds bored and lethargic, using words such as <u>inevitable</u> and <u>dreary</u>.

3. Bloom feels that a smorgasbord of possibilities creates confusion by giving students too much to choose from. However, many readers will argue that the curricula are realistic for a university interested in producing people ready for the myriad possibilities they will face in the intellectual and work force.

4. It is not true that the disciplines offered in college have little relationship to each other. For example, business administration and psychology, although they seem disparate, incorporate probability and statistics into their required course work. Environmental conservation courses incorporate lessons learned from chemical engineering, and logic relies on mathematics as a base for its theory.

5. Bloom's essay is hard to read because of its language. Whether meanings can be pulled from the context after several readings or one refers to a dictionary for words such as <u>autochonous</u>, the reader is interrupted, thereby breaking the train of thought. On the other hand it may be argued that a student is in school to be educated and frequent challenges to his vocabulary are part of that education.

6. The question posed in the first sentence is never answered and is therefore rhetorical. Bloom implies that college gives students an image of freedom from care.

<u>Writing Topics (p. 286)</u>

1. Students may be encouraged to discuss these ideas with their faculty sponsor. They may also read the student bulletin to familiarize themselves with the various courses and disciplines offered.

2. Students may wish to approach this assignment by discussing ways they've already been able to recognize that they've grown as a result of their exposure to the college environment. They can consider such aspects of that environment as classes, independent study, interaction with classmates and friends both inside and outside the classroom, intellectual and cultural programs provided by the college or university or student organizations, living situations in dorms or off-campus housing, the university community itself, and the general surroundings and society in which the school is situated. They may use friends from home who have not gone to college as a point of reference.

PRINCIPAL'S QUESTIONS

Theodore Sizer

Questions for Study and Discussion (p. 295)

1. It would take a while to coordinate lessons among
all teachers so that all disciplines are covered. It is
also not possible to change from such a system at the end of
one school year and have students come back the next year to
the new system. The school may have to continue teaching
students exposed to the old method as they had been taught
while gradually introducing the new method. Obviously
children entering school for the first time will be able to
adopt the new system.

2. Sizer's program addresses the essentials. However,
current curricula provide basics, such as home economics and
shop, to teach students practical skills as well as academic
ones. High-school-age students have a short attention span.
Seven or eight one-hour classes are more likely to hold
students' attentions than four two-hour classes. Offering
computer classes, typing, and business classes provides
students with the skills and knowledge needed to get jobs
after high school should they decide against college.

3. Many agree that it is not the school's place to
impose religion or spiritual values on students. It is up
to the parents to send children to Sunday Schools or paro-
chial schools. However, because religions have always been
so much at the center of history, they cannot be left out of
any responsible curriculum. It is possible to present them
within an historical context and to review their points of
view without presenting any one of them as final and true.

4. It is important to give as much individual attention as possible to students. Smaller classes are desirable. Rather than providing all the answers in lecture
courses, teachers should encourage students to work independently, asking their own questions and finding their own
answers.

5. In the first part, Sizer presents his plan for
improving high school education by intellectually empowering
the student. In the second part he shows that students are
not "passive receptacles," but rather choice-makers, very
much in control of the educational environment. The second
part reinforces his argument in the first part by demonstrating that educators must inspire students to learn or
they will make the choice to not learn.

6. Complicated aspects of education include the myriad
of classes, teachers, and seemingly unrelated subject areas
students must take. Social complications include the problems of peer pressure, drugs, crime, extracurricular activities, and economic status.

7. From his essay one can deduce that Sizer would
argue for individualized programs. Refer to paragraph 7 in
which Sizer answers that students should be given the task

of teaching themselves. The benefit of such a system is
that students can proceed at their own pace. For the motivated student this is beneficial; the lazy student may feel
inadequate, particularly if he/she does not receive enough
assistance.

<u>Writing Topics (p. 295)</u>

1. This assignment will require students to do some
cause and effect analysis of the influence that high school
grading systems have on students. It may be helpful to
review some of the key elements of cause and effect as they
are described in the Glossary--IMMEDIATE CAUSES, ULTIMATE
CAUSES, and CAUSAL CHAIN--and elicit some examples of how
each of these aspects might operate within the context of a
cause and effect presentation. After reviewing these
points, students may find it easier to speculate on the far-
reaching effects of grading systems on students.
2. Before students begin this writing activity, they
should review the following aspects of the argumentative
process: context, selection of details, organization, and
point-of-view.

THE AMERICAN SCHOLAR

Ralph Waldo Emerson

<u>Questions for Study and Discussion (p. 310)</u>

1. As we come from nature, to completely understand
ourselves we must study nature. But, the laws and beauty of
nature are derived from the mind--therefore, to see the
beauty and acknowledge the laws of nature is to understand
the mind that possesses these ideas.
2. Emerson capitalizes words, such as <u>Past</u>, <u>Man Think-
ing</u>, <u>Book</u>, and <u>One Man</u>, bestowing on them a heightened
importance. In the end, the scholar becomes a symbol of the
philosophical, intellectual, and spiritual leadership needed
in America.
3. Emerson refers to a fable in which a whole society
makes up "One Man." Everyone works together, yet is specialized, to get the work done for the whole society.
4. Emerson shows that all in nature is connected.
Modern disciplines such as geometry, chemistry, and science
are measurements and explanations for nature. The scholar
captures nature's beauty more so than others as he alone
sees the continuous cycle of nature and is shaped by it.
5. The three influences Emerson offers are, understanding nature, knowledge of the past through books, and
acting on intelligence. Emerson does relate "the past" with
"actions" in paragraph 22.
6. A scholar does not merely read, but applies what he
reads. Application of knowledge to his own experiences and

opinions is the key to the learning process. This is an important concept for students to learn, for many merely regurgitate texts and rarely are able to offer an individual, evolved point of view.

Writing Topics (p. 310)

1. To get a comprehensive idea about college in the 1800s, students may be able to research their school's history. If this is not possible, it may be interesting to have a history teacher familiar with this era as a guest lecturer. This may give students facts so that they can later draw conclusions on similarities and differences between then and now.

2. As a prewriting activity for this topic you can organize an informal debate around the creation/evolution argument or some other issue of your choice. First identify which students are for creation and which are for evolution, and group them accordingly. Have each group prepare for 20 minutes, gathering as much impromptu evidence as they can. When preparation is complete, you can conduct an informal debating session to air both sides of the issue. By sharing information in this way, students may find it easier to formulate opinions and supporting evidence for their own essays.

Teaching and Testing

ANGELS ON A PIN

Alexander Calandra

Questions for Study and Discussion (p. 313)

1. Calandra appears to adopt (or at least does not contradict) the student's complaint that American science and mathematics teachers do not teach the actual structure of their subjects but instead, "in a pedantic way," emphasize the nature and methods of scientific thought and the "deep inner logic" of the subject (13). An implicit, subsidiary point is that some teachers, such as Calandra's colleague, penalize students who think originally instead of parroting back the expected conventional answers (1).

2. The question was supposed to test the student's knowledge of the principles of physics, and specifically the relations between altitude and air pressure. It failed because the student, looking for an opportunity to make his point, noticed that nothing in the question referred to air pressure. Here's a revision: "Show how it is possible to determine the height of a tall building by measuring air pressure with the aid of a barometer."

3. The answer in 6 appeals most to the student probably because it is the most remote from physics--and the
funniest. He avoided the conventional answer in order "to
challenge the Sputnik-panicked classrooms of America" (13)
and the stale methods of thinking taught there.

4. Calandra begrudged the student full credit for
reasons he does not state. One may speculate that he was
accommodating his colleague, who (from paragraph 1) is less
open-minded than Calandra is. Since even on the retest the
question did not require the student to take air pressure
into account, and since the student's answer reveals if
anything a greater knowledge of physics than the conventional answer would have done, Calandra supplies no grounds for
giving less than full credit. In effect, the "system" is
"set up against the student" (1).

5. Calandra never tells us the conventional method for
determining the height of the building. He also does not
say what kind of teacher (or person) his colleague is,
information that might have suggested a more specific motive
for the student's rebellious conduct. The effect of these
omissions is to focus attention on the student's ingenuity
and on his complaint about American scientific education.

6. The essay's title, by referring to that famous
scholastic debate, suggests that the exam question too may
not only have many possible answers but be a pointless
question in the first place. (How often does one measure
the heights of buildings at all, and how often with a barometer, as opposed to surveying equipment, which would give a
more accurate answer?) The student's "scholasticism" consisted of pedantically taking the question word for word,
regardless of its context in his physics course, in order to
mock the pedantry of his instruction.

7. None of them requires a barometer to be used for
the purpose it was made to serve; another object such as a
ruler or a book would have served just as well. The answers
are therefore all contrary in spirit.

Writing Topics (p. 313)

1. The question gives interested students a lead to a
useful source: Edward de Bono, Lateral Thinking (and other
books by him). Another is James L. Adams, Conceptual Block-
busting. Lateral thinking involves finding new and unexpected uses for familiar objects (for example, using the
jagged edge of a key to open packages) or new kinds of
answers to an old problem (for example, disposing of garbage
by converting it to methane gas). De Bono and Adams provide
examples and exercises in lateral thinking, and their techniques have proven useful in scientific and corporate brainstorming.

2. This question inevitably involves the role of
evaluation and grades in education, and students will have
much to say on this topic. But tests can, of course, also
be a teaching tool, giving students the opportunity to

practice and apply what they are trying to learn. The last part of this question might be approached by setting up categories: examination questions that test students' memory of information, those that require the manipulation of data or the solving of problems, those that require students to think their way through to conclusions (as in essay examinations), and so on.

PENCILS DOWN

Andrew Ward

Questions for Study and Discussion (p. 321)

1. Ward's humor should be evident from the opening description of the dream that haunts him of having to take a final in a class he's never heard of about a subject he knows nothing about. Obviously, students' responses to Ward's use of humor may vary but they should be able to agree on a few instances where that humor is unmistakable, and examine what makes them funny.

2. Ward suggests that the pressure and approach of most testing situations offered little for him in terms of motivation or interest in subjects where there was little or no interest to begin with. He places the lack of initiative squarely on his own shoulders by admitting that outside of courses like English or History, he simply could not involve himself enough in the material to do well on tests. His use of humor helps make this point by allowing readers to laugh along with him at his lack of regard for the seriousness of testing situations, thereby indicating his doubts about their ultimate value.

3. Ward's parents are very involved in his education and very concerned when his performance doesn't measure up to their expectations. When he says that his parents had him down for college "in utero," he means that from the time even before he was born they assumed he would do well in school and go to college. It was simply a given in their plans for raising him to be a successful and happy person.

4. When he says he "couldn't read," Ward really means that as he read material he had no interest and the words made no impression and, therefore, no information was retained and no insights arrived at. This problem manifests itself in his total inability to respond to test questions that ask him to recapitulate information or ideas drawn from his reading.

5. Ward's answer for the geology exam is a continual repetition of one idea he recalls about coal from his eighth-grade science class. The answer is mainly inadequate because he makes no mention of information he was supposed to learn in his Geology course.

Ward may have fared better with this type of writing in a nonscientific course because there would be less emphasis on recapitulating information remembered from the course and more on presenting a discussion and from his own point of view, relying on his own observations and experiences to support his answer. This may be the reason why he usually did better in English and History than in courses like Geology.

Ward organizes his material chronologically, beginning with the first real test he can remember and working his way through a variety of test-taking experiences in grade school and high school, and finishing with his last final at Oberlin.

Paragraphs 1-6 fit into the organizational structure by beginning at a point after the last disastrous exam at Oberlin, to establish his main idea about the sense of anxiety and failure he associates with test-taking situations.

7. Students' responses to this question will likely focus on the different manner and variety of ways in which we are tested outside the academic community, but they will no doubt also agree that the specific written response to materials learned, as described in Ward's essay, is a type of examination pretty much confined to the academic world.

Writing Topics (p. 321)

1. As a prewriting activity for this topic you can discuss with students the specific nature of their college entrance examinations and their responses to these situations. By examining both the positive and negative aspects that students can remember in regard to their College Boards, they may find it easier to formulate their opinions about the efficacy of such tests in the admissions process.

2. A discussion of issues related to evaluating student progress usually breaks down into an analysis of grades and their role in the educational process. As a prewriting activity, therefore, you can discuss with students what importance they feel should be attached to the assigning of grades, and what effect grades have in evaluating and motivating students. Such a discussion may help them determine the value or feasibility of any alternatives to traditional academic testing they may devise.

3. A close look at Ward's description of his reading and studying for the geology exam may be a good starting point for discussing some of the issues that inhibit students from doing well on tests. You might also try establishing, in class, what Ward could have done to more adequately prepare for the exam, particularly after he recognized that he "was reduced to hoping that it was all penetrating [his] mind subconsciously" (34).

LEARNING TO SEE

Samuel H. Scudder

<u>Questions for Study and Discussion (p. 326)</u>

1. As Scudder reveals in paragraphs 25 and 26, the
best entomological lesson he ever received was Professor
Agassiz's repeated injunction to simply "Look, look, look."
From it Scudder learned of the inestimable value of "observing facts and their orderly arrangement" (31) and then
bringing them "into connection with some general law" (32).
2. Agassiz's method forces the student to depend upon
his own initiative and capacity to see in making discoveries
and then placing them within the wider context of their
applications to science and nature. It works with Scudder
because of his innate sense of curiosity and his strong
desire to find answers that will satisfy himself and his
instructor.
Students' opinions on whether such a method of teaching
would be effective today will depend on the degree to which
they believe students in general are inquisitive and self-
motivated.
3. Scudder studied haemulons for eight months, an
amount of time necessary for the slow process of observation
and review described in the essay. Students' opinions on
whether the process could have been speeded up with the use
of lectures and/or textbooks may vary. Many may allow that
it could have been done faster, but to an ultimately less
comprehensive and less effective outcome.
4. Scudder hits upon the idea of drawing the fish only
after exhausting what he then felt were all other possibilities in simply looking at it. When he does draw it, though,
he begins to discover new features as the process of drawing
focuses his attention and concentration more closely to what
he is observing. This kind of sharpening of the powers of
observation is what Agassiz refers to when he says "a pencil
is one of the best eyes."
5. Though Scudder looks back on his first encounter
with Professor Agassiz as the most important entomological
lesson he ever had, as he was actually experiencing it he
was not too pleased. Words and phrases that contribute to
this sense of displeasure include: <u>aversion</u> (8); <u>disap-
pointment</u>, <u>did not commend itself to an ardent entomologist</u>,
<u>I had seen all that could be seen</u>, <u>lingering</u>, <u>this little
excitement over</u>, <u>nothing was to be done</u>, <u>loathsome</u>, <u>ghastly</u>,
<u>despair</u>, <u>infinite relief</u>, <u>I was free</u> (9); <u>hideous</u>, <u>feeling
of desperation</u>, <u>nonsense</u> (10); <u>piqued</u>, <u>mortified</u> (16);
<u>disconcerting</u>, <u>perplexities</u> (20).
Overall, the style and diction of Scudder's essay is
formal and academic, and is apparent right away in the first
paragraph. Though such style and diction is appropriate for
the subject matter, the level of formality does, at times,
suggest that the essay was written in the previous century.

The following samples of diction are the most obvious clues
to the essay's age: my antecedents, purposed (1); eau-de-
Cologne (8); interdicted (10).
        6. Agassiz's statement suggests that there is no real
reason to "Look, look, look" and digest or record the results of such observation unless those results can teach you
something about general principles of science and nature;
otherwise you will simply be filling your head with useless
information.

Writing Topics (p. 326)

        1. As a prewriting activity you can tie discussion of
this topic to consideration of study question 2 above. By
looking closely at the approach Professor Agassiz uses to
teach Scudder "to see," and then discussing whether such a
method would work as well today, students may be better
prepared to analyze the influence that an effective teacher
has had on them, and how that influence was affected by
their own levels of inquisitiveness and ambition.
        2. To demonstrate how the pencil can act as one of the
best of eyes, you can ask students to do a 10-15 minute
freewriting session in which they respond to Professor
Agassiz's or Anne Morrow Lindbergh's comment. When they've
finished writing, have them read their responses aloud and
then discuss with them what, if anything, they discovered
about writing and its relationship to thinking as a result
of this short freewriting exercise.
        3. This topic will doubtless provoke a lively debate
over educational methods, such as quizzes and multiple-
choice exams. The fact is, however, that in much of life
people are required to answer others' questions, whether a
superior's about the reason for declining widget production
or a child's about the beginning of the universe, and in
this respect answering the teachers' questions is practice
for real life. There are also, of course, many fields in
which students learn how to ask questions, fields ranging
from the sciences to philosophy, and all subjects have their
own methodologies which, among other things, define what
kinds of questions are relevant and answerable using the
methods of the discipline. The discussion might be turned
to this area by asking students what majors or careers they
have in mind and what role question-asking plays in those
majors and careers.

THEME FOR ENGLISH B

Langston Hughes

Questions for Study and Discussion (p. 329)

        1. The instructor is saying, in effect, "Write about
what you know." The result can then be "true"--that is,

based on personal experience and conviction, therefore well-grounded and sincere.

2.   The student has much in common with Hughes, as the headnote to the poem reveals, but there are differences: the student was born in Winston-Salem, North Carolina, and is twenty-two, while Hughes was born in Joplin, Missouri, and was nineteen when he attended Columbia. Once your students have discovered these distinctions, a productive discussion might follow on why Hughes chose to use such a speaker--or any speaker at all.

3.   First, Columbia University _is_ on a hill and Harlem is not. But the reference has other significances: the University offers a way up and out of the poverty of the African-American ghetto; the University is also distanced from the lives of Harlem African-Americans, as lines 34-35 and line 10 suggest, and doubtless most of those who teach and study at Columbia consider themselves socially as well as intellectually "above" Harlem.

4.   The student and instructor are "part of" each other in two respects: at the moment each is part of the other's life, and more generally each stands for an aspect of American life which shapes the society in which both live and therefore helps to define the character of each. In this sense, we are indeed all part of each other.

5.   The answer to this question depends mainly on what course we think "English B" is. We think it is Freshman Composition, or at least a prose writing course, because in a poetry-writing course the instructor would not ask for "a page," and therefore a poem such as this one would not be what the instructor wanted. However, it does fulfill the specific requirements of the assignment, for it is about a page long and clearly "comes out of" the student.

Writing Topics (p. 330)

1.   Fundamentally this discussion turns upon the students' view of education as it is and as it should be. Teachers who learn from their students generally conceive of education as a process, a dialogue. The essays of Emerson, Calandra, Ward, and Scudder directly or indirectly describe teachers or styles of teaching. As a focus for the discussion, you may want to ask students to consider what if anything the teachers in each of those articles learn from their students.

2.   Students generally enjoy this topic, with its implicit opportunity to criticize the writing assignments they have previously been given in this and other courses. However, they also discover that inventing stimulating and workable assignments is not as easy as they might have thought! In preparatory discussion you might invite the students to consider such factors as the purpose of their assignments, what kinds of results are desired and how they are to be judged, and the requirement that an assignment be intelligible to and manageable by a heterogeneous class such

as their own. (The obvious follow-up to this topic is to
ask students to write essays on the assignments they think
are the best.)

THE LESSON

Toni Cade Bambara

Questions for Study and Discussion (p. 337)

     1. Sylvia and her friends laugh at Miss Moore because
she is different. She is also educated, which may threaten
Sylvia, her friends and family.
     2. Sylvia is angry at society for the differences
among its members. She sees the upper class as being responsible for the poverty of the lower classes.
     3. Bambara uses the following words to describe Miss
Moore: nappy, proper, hated, spooky, boring-ass, dog,
bitch, nosy. Sylvia is jealous of Miss Moore for being
richer and better educated than Sylvia and her family are.
     4. Miss Moore feels that it is her responsibility as
an educated person to teach the children about the world.
"The Lesson" is not only Miss Moore "teaching" the children
about money, but more importantly, Sylvia learning something
about herself. The significance of the title, although
apparent in the end, does not seem to have significance in
the beginning.
     5. The last paragraph shows that "The Lesson" has been
learned despite Sylvia's negative attitude. Readers also
learn that it is possible to gain wisdom from common occurrences.

Writing Topics (p. 337)

     1. The students who truly benefit from this assignment
will be able to make a general statement about life based on
their own personal experiences. The observations needn't be
brand new to be insightful. It may be interesting to share
the results with the class to prove that general statements
about life can be found in everyday occurrences.
     2. Students should be able to clearly show what their
own lifestyle is like. It may be helpful for the students
to review the section on DICTION in the Glossary, as this
will help relay character. It may be interesting to pass
the final copies among the class and ask the group to guess
which student each paper is describing.

THE UNROMANTIC GENERATION

Bruce Weber

<u>Questions for Study and Discussion (p. 348)</u>

1. Weber wanted to find out if recent college graduates are as cynical and materialistic as they are imagined
to be by the rest of society. He expected to find among
young adults traits similar to those his generation exhibit-
ed when the were in their twenties. As he says in paragraph
12, he felt he would be "plumbing a little of my past."
Instead, Weber found logical and practical planners.
2. Weber is admiring of the new young generation as
evidenced in words and phrases such as "News conscious,"
"media smart," "sophisticated," "distinct," "planners,"
"they have priorities," "They are not heartless, soulless,
cold or unimaginative." Weber does make reference to them
being "self-preoccupied," but defends them by saying all
"youthful generations have always been," and that this
generation is finally aware of it.
3. Weber defines his control group in paragraph 8 as
"between the ages of twenty-two and twenty-six, graduated
from college, are living in or around an urban center, and
are heterosexual . . . they are planners." These people
differ in their views about marriage, but basically agree
that it is inevitable. This group is not representative of
today's youth on the whole, excluding as it does the working
class, those who marry right out of high school and pursue
an education later, and those who go to college, fall in
love and then quit. For the group it represents, this study
does seem to accurately represent the goals and determination of today's graduate.
4. Young people look for monogamy, practicality, and a
relationship that will not threaten their financial stability or career.
5. Weber explains that the threat of AIDS has led to
diminishing sexual promiscuity. "Forecasts of economic
doom," housing problems, and the "chaotic" future have young
people wanting to establish themselves before marriage and
maintain their careers afterwards.
6. Weber implies that because of the changing world,
the younger generation is acting in a way essential to their
financial stability and health. They fear that promiscuity
will lead to AIDS and STDs. Illogical, impractical career
choices may lead to undesirable financial situations.
However, practical thinking may be boring and the high
standards it demands may lead to burn out.
7. Weber defines a young persons' view of romance as
"inevitable" and "restricting." However, first he presents
sufficient examples, quotes and theories to support this

statement so that when he finally utters it, it rings true.

8.   When Weber speaks of AIDS as the thing that will bring back romance in the younger generation, he points to the chilling thought that the specter of death and not more benevolent forces might inspire romance.

Writing Topics (p. 349)

1.   Before beginning this essay, it may be beneficial for students to review the basics of organization so they can group the information they collect in a manner effective for their argument.

2.   Students will find research materials in the library under the subject headings <u>Love</u> and <u>Marriage</u>. Of the recent books alluded to in the questioning, we mean in particular those of Ernest Van Den Haag, beginning with <u>The Invention That Isn't Working</u>.

DATE RAPE: THE STORY OF AN EPIDEMIC AND THOSE WHO DENY IT

Ellen Sweet

Questions for Study and Discussion (p. 358)

1.   See paragraph 16 for the empty excuses given by schools for a failure to investigate date rape. One school could not invest the time in such a study, because they do not have the time to invest in the possible results of the study. Should it be learned that rape is occurring with a greater frequency than generally known, schools would jeopardize their good name and be forced to spend time on programming about "Date Rape." This is also the case for the school who "doesn't want to be left holding the bag." But what do they really fear? Perhaps they underestimate the depth of the problem and the maturity of the students. "Limited foreseeable benefit," "We don't want to get involved," and "too volatile a subject" are remarks that reveal an "ignore-it-and-it-will-go-away" attitude.

2.   Crafts denies the problem by assuming that female Brandeis students only date within the university. The town of Waltham, where Brandeis is located, is a suburb of Boston. It is near several other colleges and there is a Boston train that makes two stops in the town. Brandeis students are not the only males in the area. Crafts also assumes that low intelligence is a factor in rape offenders, while studies show that violent crime, including sexual assault, is not linked to I.Q.

3.   In attempts to raise doubts about the character of the victim and the guilt of the rapist, defense attorneys for the rapists ask questions regarding the victim's virginity, her family sexual history, her sexual preference, fashion habits, and prior relations with the rapist. The assumption is that something about the victim may have made

her in some way responsible for the attack.

4. Although Sweet does follow this solution with, "and men clearly need to believe them more," Sweet is still placing some of the responsibility on the victim. What more does a woman need to say after she has said, "NO"?

5. Each rape victim said she "could not believe" it happened to her. Few women would expect to be raped by someone they know and like well enough to date. Sweet is trying to point out that it could happen to anyone. In addition to these accounts of victims, Sweet cites studies on the problem (Koss, Burkhart), quotes authorities who have worked in rape crisis centers, explains the reluctance of many schools to participate in research on date rape, and shows what's being done to address the problem.

6. No, it does not. However, Resken's point is that many jurors still assume that date rape is sexually-motivated rather than an act of aggression.

7. The crime of rape may go unreported for a combination of the following reasons: a victim feels no one would believe her; she hesitates to turn in a person of the same social circle; she wants to forget about it; she knows what she will face if she goes to court; she may feel responsible; and she may feel people will judge and blame her.

Writing Topics (p. 358)

1. As a prewriting activity you may have the students list the qualities of a college that would lend itself to a high exposure to rape. You can help facilitate the discussion as to whether campuses are more at risk. If the students agree that colleges do have a responsibility to address the issue, you may want students to consider what the school can do. If the school has a rape awareness/prevention program, students could obtain information from them about what their school is doing about the problem.

2. As a prewriting activity for this assignment you may ask the students to think of a time when they have told a lie so untrue that they had to tell more lies so the truth would not come out. As the lies escalated was the original lie forgotten? Or did the student eventually believe the initial lie? Taking this approach may make the student realize that by skirting the issue some people are lying to themselves and the effects may be the same. Students will also want to think about the improvements in a situation that usually occur as a result of public awareness.

COLLEGE IS A WASTE OF TIME AND MONEY

Caroline Bird

1. Bird summarizes her reasons for believing college a waste of time and money in paragraphs 53-56: 1) college doesn't make people intelligent, ambitious, happy, or liberal; 2) college can't claim much credit for the learning experiences that really change students; 3) even motivated students are disappointed with their college courses and professors; and 4) a college diploma no longer opens as many vocational doors.
   Students' responses to these reasons may vary.
2. In her first paragraph Bird states that the majority of college students are in school "because it has become the thing to do or because college is a pleasant place to be; because it's the only way they can get parents or taxpayers to support them without working at a job they don't like; because Mother wanted them to go, or some other reason totally irrelevant to the course of studies for which college is supposedly organized."
   Students' reactions to Bird's assessment may vary, and discussion of this question in class can yield some lively debate.
3. Bird believes students now protest "individually rather than in concert," by turning inward and withdrawing from active participation. As a result, those who feel discontent often opt to drop out and travel, or "refuse to go to college at all . . . [or] simply hang around college unhappily and reluctantly" (8). Students' opinions on whether this is accurate for their campus may vary, though most will probably recognize particular cases where Bird's assessment is applicable.
4. According to Bird, "students are sad because they are not needed." The work force is already overcrowded and so "there is no room for so many newly minted 18-year-olds each year" (12).
   Students' responses to this evaluation may vary. Some may take issue with the central premise that students are, in fact, sad.
5. Bird recognizes "there is a certain unreality to the game" because she knows that parents do not hand over the money for college in one lump sum, and because she understands that financial considerations are rarely the sole criteria for sending children to college. As she states in paragraph 29, "Quite aside from the noneconomic benefits of college, and these should loom larger once the dollars are cleared away, there are grave difficulties in assigning a dollar value to college at all."
   Students' responses to Bird's belief that "few parents are sophisticated enough to understand that . . . their children would be better off with the money than with the

education" may vary. This is another question that can serve as the focus for lively debate in class.

6. Bird quotes an economic dictionary to explain that "psychic income" is "'income that is reckoned in terms of pleasure, satisfaction, or general feelings of euphoria'" (37). More generally, it is simply the "nonmonetary rewards of work." People can estimate the value of psychic income by measuring the importance they attach to being happy and content in the work they do, regardless of the amount of money they make.

Students will no doubt recognize the value of psychic income for all individuals, but the degree to which they ascribe it importance may vary.

7. The "new vocationalism" Bird refers to is the recognition on behalf of college administrators and professors that one of the basic purposes of education is career preparation, and so they've begun to place an emphasis on the "ethic of achievement and service" in addition to the more traditional idealistic goals of higher education. Students will probably agree that this attitude remains a campus reality in the 80's.

8. Bird uses a wide range of sources to substantiate her argument. In addition to the general description, in paragraph 11, of how she went about her research, she cites the following specific sources to lend credibility to the individual points she raises: 1) economist Fritz Machlup; 2) educator Nevitt Sanford; 3) The Carnegie Commission; 4) Richard Baloga, a policeman's son; 5) Sol Linowitz, once chairman of the American Council on Education; 6) author Daniel Yankelovich; 7) Leon Lefkowitz, social studies chairman at Central High School in Valley Stream, N.Y.; 8) a sociologist; 9) Stephen G. Necel, a young banker in Poughkeepsie, N.Y.; 10) Christopher Jencks, author of _Inequality_; 11) Jacob Mincer, of the National Bureau of Economic Research and Columbia University; 12) The Department of Labor; 13) Jerry Darling, an Indianapolis man who returned to school after working a number of years; 14) 30 Vassar psychology majors; 15) John Shingleton, director of placement at Michigan State University; 16) The American Enterprise Institute; 17) Charles Lawrence, producer of a Chicago television show; and 18) Glenn Bassett, personnel specialist at G.E.

The sheer number and variety of sources represented here, together with the information elicited from them, argue against Bird merely being opinionated, cynical, or sensational.

9. Paragraphs 52-57 summarize the issues Bird has elaborated upon in her essay. They are an effective conclusion because they organize the points in almost list fashion, helping readers put them into a combined and coherent perspective when finishing the essay. This is not possible in the body of the essay because of the discussion and explanation that accompany each point.

1. As a prewriting activity for this topic you can discuss with students what their acquaintances from high school who did not go to school are currently doing. As part of your discussion, have students examine how valuable the examples presented might be as "possible learning experiences and opportunities for personal growth." This may help students formulate their opinions about the range of alternative learning experiences available to them.

2. As a prewriting discussion for this topic you can explore the degree to which both essays focus on the financial rewards of college to the exclusion of other benefits of higher education. Both Gardner and Bird seem preoccupied with success in the marketplace, Gardner as a nation and Bird as individuals. Find out if students believe either or both go overboard in this emphasis and, if so, to the detriment of what other factors? Your discussion may help them recognize other points of similarity or difference in the two essays as well.

3. It may be worthwhile to share the results of this assignment with students, particularly if they have sensed an overemphasis on financial concerns in Bird's analysis of the value of a college education.

OUR SCHOOLS FOR SCANDAL

George F. Will

Questions for Study and Discussion (p. 372)

1. In paragraph 3 Will explains that athletes have been shuffled through school, insulated from expectations, and "they have spent four years acquiring the idea that they are exempt from normal standards," and as a consequence are "less suited" for society.

2. High schools are largely at fault for the athlete scandal by refusing to establish "no pass, no play" rules. The attitude that the athlete is exempt is initiated in high school. In college the young athlete enters a vicious cycle already in progress in which pressure is put on the coach, by parents, alumni and administration, to win. Every win brings more spectators to the next game and therefore more money. Every win also brings the team closer to bowl games which bring in even more money and fame. Some coaches come to have good reason to believe that bending a few rules is worth the end result, when their jobs are on the line. However, it is always the athlete who is left holding the bag after his four years of eligibility are over. As Will says (paragraph 4), college is "the end of the road for most student athletes."

3. The title "Our Schools for Scandal" is taken from R. B. Sheridan's comedy The School for Scandal produced in

1777. This comedy of manners satirizes the sanctimonious-
ness, pretentions, and frivolity of fashionable English
society. In the end honesty and goodness win the day.

4. Will begins by quoting coaches who joke about the
scandal of college sports. He then outlines the problems
and consequences of the system and concludes with suggestions for change. Will could have organized his essay
differently. It might have been easier to read if Will had
presented the advantages of school athletics at the beginning, then listed the sacrifices made in order to win, then
shown how this is to the athlete's disadvantage, and then
offered a solution.

5. Will's defense of college athletics does not weaken
his argument. On the contrary, readers will be able to
discern as he has that it is not sports themselves, but the
greed and wanton disregard for the athletes that are at the
heart of the problem. By allowing for what is good about
sports, Will can be seen as a reasonable, thinking critic
instead of a fanatic railing against a treasured American
phenomenon.

6. Will wants something to be done about the deplor-
able state of college athletics. His offer of solutions
makes it clear he intends to persuade the reader into action. His essay is intended for a wide audience, since a
broad spectrum of people can be said to share responsibility
for the state of affairs, including parents, teacher, coaches, the administration, and alumni.

7. The quotes Will uses perpetuate the cynical attitude towards the issue and help Will build his argument that
something needs to be done.

8. Sports programs prosper by exploiting the dreams of
ghetto children at the expense of their educations. If
Will's suggestions were enforced, fewer African-Americans
might be admitted to college on full scholarships.

Writing Topics (p. 373)

1. In writing about causes and effects, students
should keep in mind the requirement that a cause or causes
must be both sufficient and necessary to bring a purported
effect. You may want to take one of the example topics and
list some causes and effects in class to facilitate the type
of thinking needed for this essay.

2. In addition to building convincing arguments, students will need to utilize the elements of informational
process analysis while they organize their information. It
may therefore be helpful for the students to review the
entry for PROCESS ANALYSIS in the Glossary at the back of
the book.

SON OF ANIMAL HOUSE

Chris Miller

Questions for Study and Discussion (p. 380)

1. Miller uses the following fraternity related words: brothers, drop our pants, booted, mooning, pledge, Night of Seven Fires, Green Key Weekend, rush, run a rack, chug, dip, lunch meat, hooking, ding, hazing, and Bacchanalian. This terminology brings the reader closer to the subject and establishes the writer's authority. The absence of this terminology would make the discussion seem less real and, therefore, less persuasive.

2. In paragraph 6, Miller says that the release of Animal House "coincided with and perhaps contributed to the rebound of fraternities."

3. Miller does not defend fraternities on the basis of the moral or educational characteristics of their members. He simply believes and argues that there is a place for this type of organization on college campuses.

4. Miller feels animal behavior is a rebellion of a sort, against a student's proper upbringing. Some students will agree. However, others will argue that they are merely too immature to take care of themselves. Many of them never had to do their own laundry and feel burdened by that and a host of other new responsibilities. Freedom from parents and the availability of alcohol also excites students into previously uncharacteristic behavior.

5. In paragraph 7, the administration, faculty, Trustees, and police are presented as opposed to the Greek System. They argue that fraternities interfere "with college life and the health and well-being of students." They also point to "sexism, and elitism, and conformity and anti-intellectual hedonism."

Writing Topics (p. 381)

1. As a prewriting activity for this assignment you may "choose a side" and show students how the opening paragraph for each could be approached. For example, the attack for college sponsored activities could begin by showing the bad aspects as increased student fees, but the defense can argue that these events give students an alternative to drinking and partying.

2. As a prewriting activity you could hold an informal debate with those opposed to the Greek system and those who would like to maintain the system. This exposure to the subject may help students formulate and organize their ideas for their essays.

Media and Advertising

ADVERTISING'S FIFTEEN BASIC APPEALS

Jib Fowles

Questions for Study and Discussion (p. 401)

    1. We do not agree that buyers have become stoutly
resistant to advertisements. Buyers are aware, to a certain
extent, of the morals being inflicted on them and some of
the emotions being appealed to. But, there are some appeals
and claims that buyers are not aware of. We find that
Shrank and Rosenbaum are convincing enough in their arguments to make readers aware of how frequently they are
fooled. Students will no doubt have many examples of their
own gullibility.
    2. Fowles's tone must seem somewhat overbearing to the
student unfamiliar with psychology. His references to some
of the great psychologists would mean nothing to such a
reader. Although Fowles seems proud of his discovery of
fifteen appeals, readers get lost in the process. Still,
they may question Fowles's downgrading of the works of
Maslow, Murray, and McClelland.
    3. In Fowles's extensive explanation of the process
that went into finding his appeals, he borrows ideas from
well-known psychologists. He also uses many examples to
support his thesis. He is convincing as a professor who
knows a great deal about psychology; however he tempers that
knowledge by refuting thinkers who are at least as well-
respected as he is. We do not find all of his examples to
be thoroughly convincing.
    4. The emotional appeal is found in the artwork.
    5. Fowles suggests that Florence Henderson is the main
appeal in Wesson Oil commercials, although the food plays an
equally major role. The sight of fried chicken and French
fries soaking in Wesson Oil appeals to a simple, basic need,
the desire for good, hot, greasy food. Most food ads rely
on the sight of mouth-watering food to make the sale.
Fowles's assessment of ad writers' intentions may be correct; however it is possible that consumers are perhaps not
so easily influenced. More than any other product, food is
subject to tests which have an immediate and definite influence over the consumer. They are less likely to be fooled
just because it is endorsed by a perceived motherly image or
has a history.
    6. Although public protest has at times forced adver-
tisers to pull campaigns, mere opposition to an ad might not
necessarily bring it to a halt, unless, of course, that
opposition affects sales. Ad writers may be satisfied with

91

ads which get attention, good or bad; publicity is the whole idea.

<u>Writing Topics (p. 402)</u>

1.   It may be helpful for students to get more information on subliminal advertising before beginning this assignment. Students can find additional information under the heading <u>Subliminal Advertising</u> in the library's subject catalogue or various indexes.
2.   As a prewriting activity you may review the elements of division and classification for this assignment. Once the assignment is complete you may want to share some of the more witty responses with the entire class.

THE HARD SELL

Ron Rosenbaum

<u>Questions for Study and Discussion (p. 413)</u>

1.   Rosenbaum describes the Hard Sell era of the fast-talking salesman. This was the "no more Mr. Nice Guy" school of commercial strategy, or the "take-it-or-leave-it approach." Hard Life commercials contain hard, fast facts and an emphasis on the idea that life is tough, which leads in turn to the need for tough products. For example, Dodge trucks are "ram tough," and Ford trucks are "built tough." The Humiliation Sell suggests that consumers had better use deodorant that works overtime and a detergent that removes "ring around the collar," so they will not embarrass themselves in public. Rosenbaum is not opposed to love in advertising as long as it is cuddly and emotional. He is opposed to the materialistic "murder [being] committed" in some commercials as in the case of the poor husband who was chastised for not buying his wife a Longines for Christmas.
2.   Rosenbaum uses words such as <u>us</u>, <u>we</u>, and <u>our</u>, in an attempt to relate to the reader more personally. In this way Rosenbaum includes himself in the pool of humanity that is subjected to the tactics used by ad writers.
3.   Ad writers exploit the idea that life is tough so that manufacturers can assume the role of savior when they produce products that make life easier. In this tough life, we can turn to the makers of Excedrin to relieve our headaches, and the makers of heavy duty paper products to quicken dinner clean up.
4.   Rosenbaum does not like the Hard Sell ads. In paragraph six he calls them the "no nonsense ads." Nor does he like the "Aching '80s" or "Bull Apart" ads as evidenced in his sarcastic suggestion that the bull of yesterday's brokerage advertisement has suffered PBB poisoning or cattle mutations. It is, however, obvious that Rosenbaum does like "happy ads." In paragraph 25 he uses words such as <u>warmth</u>,

spiritual, <u>camaraderie</u>, <u>lyrical</u>, and <u>beauty</u>, which contrast with words such as <u>abruptly</u>, <u>survival</u>, <u>combative</u>, <u>anger</u>, <u>assault</u>, <u>dank</u>, and <u>lonely</u> used in the rest of the essay.

5.   Rosebaum's vocabulary and tone indicate that his audience is mature, educated and sophisticated. He uses words such as <u>sophistry</u>, <u>concierge</u>, <u>insidious</u>, and <u>malleable</u>, and discusses investments and refers to Renoir's painting of Louis XVI. Fowles' diction tends to be less formal and in places more colloquial. And like Rosenbaum he freely uses jargon from the worlds of advertising and psychology. Fowles' article appeared in an academic journal and was intended for an audience similar to Rosenbaum's.

Writing Topics (p. 413)

1.   As a prewriting activity you may conduct a class discussing politics, industry, education, and family in the 1990s. You can have the students speculate on the differences and the courses of change. You may also be able to obtain magazines of the past and compare the ads to today's ads to show the progression of change. This may help students to organize their ideas for this assignment.

2.   To facilitate this assignment and make it more immediate, it may be helpful to provide students with a videotape of various commercials that address the topics Rosenbaum discusses.

NOW . . . THIS

Neil Postman

Questions for Study and Discussion (p. 424)

1.   The words "Now . . . this" are frightening to Postman because no matter how serious the information that comes after them, they are uttered "without knitted brow--indeed with a kind of idiot's delight." "Now . . . this" has become a new conjunction which separates everything from everything, according to Postman, and as such is a metaphor for the discontinuity of thoughts and ideas that are the content of "conversation" in present-day America. It confirms the media belief that thoughts that follow each other need not be related. In other words, the world has no meaning or order. Television time is perfect for this "Now . . . this" world view because it is already broken into short segments both to allow for commercial breaks and to keep the viewer from dwelling too long on any single thought.

2.   "Hampered viewer acceptance" means simply that "viewers do not like looking at the performer" either because he or she is unattractive or because he or she is not credible. In theatrical terms this means that the viewer is

not persuaded that the performer is the character being portrayed.

3. Postman distinguishes a "reality truth" as one which can be judged to be true or not true based on empirical observation. The other "new" kind of truth evident on broadcast news is based on the performer's giving the "impression of sincerity, authenticity, vulnerability, or attractiveness."

4. In paragraphs 6 and 7 Postman asks a series of questions designed to get the reader thinking about the meaning of "truth" as interpreted by television news producers. He expects the reader to answer "yes" to all his questions, which makes the reader his ally in his concern over the nature of television "truth." In paragraph 10 Postman asks the reader to question the necessity for music on a news broadcast. This question and others like it in the essay force readers to question elements of a news show they take for granted. In paragraph 19 Postman "quizzes" readers to let them see for themselves how little they actually "learn" from the news.

5. News shows spend no more than forty-five seconds on any news story, thus preventing the viewer from taking them seriously. Film footage provides easy diversion. News casters reveal little emotion or reaction to the stories they report so as not to alarm or otherwise upset the viewer. Frequent commercial breaks discharge the negative feelings a report may arouse in viewers. All news shows have musical themes.

6. Postman's example of the Burger King break after the nuclear war announcement will seem exaggerated only to students who never watch television news. Most readers will find it an effective example because it recalls the blunt interruption of hard facts they experience every time they tune in the nightly report.

7. In his constant use of the words "you" and "we" Postman adopts the reader (and also the television viewer) as his ally and confidant. However, his description of the successful tactic that television news uses suggests the television producers may be right about their audience. For example, "as long as the music is there as a frame for the program, the viewer is comforted to believe that there is nothing to be greatly alarmed about" (10). Postman paints television news producers as deceivers who, rightly or wrongly, have a low opinion of an American viewing public which does not want to be troubled by reality. For example, "Viewers are rarely required to carry over any thought or feeling from one parcel of time to another" (3). "It is also considerable help in maintaining a high level of unreality that the newscasters do not pause to grimace or shiver when they speak of their prefaces or epilogues to the film clips" (12).

8. Postman predicts that our culture will not survive the trivialization of news. That is, if we do not take

world events more seriously and give them the attention they merit, we will suffer the consequences of our own ignorance.

Writing Topics (p. 424)

1. Students may wish to use examples of the new, popular societal interest news shows such as "Unsolved Mysteries" and "911." You may use a class discussion to have students discern how these shows present their stories and whether it is with more or less theatrics than the regular 6:00 news. You may also have the students think about how these shows contribute to the mentality that Postman discusses. Do these shows make light of the tragedies and crimes occurring by devoting an hour-long slot to them during prime time?

2. All call-in shows are not the same. Some are "frivolous" while others may be more informative. Ask students to be sure to sample shows from a variety of sources, such as educational television and radio as well as the commercial stations. Ask students to consider how these sources differ in their goals and approaches in the dispensing of information.

3. As a prewriting activity you may collect some clippings about the tearing down of the Berlin Wall or about the 1990 Iraqi invasion of Kuwait (and the taking of Western hostages as "human shields") since some students may not be familiar with these stories. This may give students the incentive to investigate their own stories for their essays. You may suggest certain periodical indexes available to the students in the library.

ADVERTISING IN DISGUISE: HOW THE HIDDEN HAND OF A CORPORATE GHOSTWRITER CAN TURN A NEWS REPORT INTO A COMMERCIAL

Consumer Reports

Questions for Study and Discussion (p. 432)

1. A news story carries the weight of truth to the average viewer and so is more valuable than advertising to a corporation. However, it is the function of the news media to present unbiased reporting of business stories and that function is imperiled when the distinction between news and ads is blurred.

2. The Report describes four ways that P.R. firms have honed their canning techniques.

P.R. firms offer "canned" stories to the networks, or local reporters can "voice over" silent, canned material. Agencies provide the names of local retailers of their product which can be added to the packaged report to give it local appeal. "The vanishing interviewer" trick allows a local station to dub the face or voice of one of its own reporters over the footage of an interview that has been conducted by a P.R. person. "In effect, the reporter serves as an actor in a commercial." Footage is packaged in video cassette form or can be beamed in via satellite.

3. The lengthy illustrations are necessary to describe the methods, motives and effects of these ad campaigns.

4. Canned news appears in the special sections of newspapers, such as those covering real estate, automobiles, travel, and food. The commercial plug usually is "buried" so readers will mistake the "ad" for a feature article. Most articles of this kind run in papers with a circulation under 80,000. Large papers sometimes run canned news for big advertisers. The more ads a paper sells, the more news stories it can afford to run. If a paper lacks genuine news stories, it sometimes fills extra space with "canned" news.

5. Some students may answer that "business is business." Others may answer that they were struck by the "shameless" tone of the response of the P.R. people.

6. Consumer Reports is written for the average consumer as is evidenced by the use of a reasonable vocabulary, clear, interesting illustrations, and to-the-point quotes from both sides of the issue. For example, the first six paragraphs ask nothing of readers but that they hear the story of one ad campaign that was used as a news story.

7. The thesis is stated in paragraph 6: "by blurring the distinction between news and advertising, such activities imperil an important function of the media: providing consumers with accurate, unbiased information about the marketplace."

Writing Topics (p. 433)

1. As students watch news stories about products, they will also want to pay attention to the way real ads attempt to simulate news stories. Have students keep in mind the elements necessary to a good news story, to a good ad. Are any of them interchangeable?

2. Students need to keep in mind the elements of a good news story. Suggest that a member of class contact the campus newspaper for a rundown of those elements. Included should be aspects of objectivity, conciseness, a strong lead, and balanced reporting.

3. Refer students to the glossary of the text for the highlights of several different means of presenting readers with their point of view, such as ARGUMENT, CAUSE AND EFFECT and DEFINITION.

96

Prejudice and Sexism

THE LANGUAGE OF PREJUDICE

Gordon Allport

Questions for Study and Discussion (p. 444)

1. Allport states his main idea most directly in paragraph 3: "The very act of classifying forces us to overlook all other features, many of which might offer a sounder basis than the rubric we select." Allport's supporting argument may be summarized as follows: first, he demonstrates the effect of certain commonly used, apparently innocently descriptive words which actually function as "symbols of primary potency" (blind, Chinese, Jew) and block out our awareness of a person's other characteristics. Allport then examines the negative connotations which categorizing words often carry, whether deliberately or through their cultural associations. As a case in point, he traces the use of the label "communist" in America after World War I, showing that it functioned as a "verbal symbol" to discredit a certain element of society. Finally, through two historical examples, Allport shows that mere words can arouse as powerful a reaction as their referents.

2. Though nouns are essential tools in "clustering" our perceptions, Allport notes that "each label we use, especially those of primary potency, distracts our attention from concrete reality" (6) and "magnifies one attribute all out of proportion to its true significance, and masks other important attributes of the individual . . . " (7).

3. Labels of primary potency, says Allport, "act like shrieking sirens, deafening us to all find discriminations that we might otherwise perceive" (4); that is, they are particularly capable of causing us to view a person as a stereotype rather than as a complex individual with a host of different attributes. Though such labels may sometimes be unavoidable, their force can be greatly diminished by changing them from nouns into adjectives (9).

4. Depending on the part of the country they are from, some students may be surprised or amused at some of Allport's examples. For example, where anti-Catholic prejudice is unknown the term papist will hardly have much emotional impact. On the other hand, seeing words like nigger, wop, and kike in print (11) always has shock value, and emphasizes Allport's point about the qualitative difference between such words and the more neutral Negro, Italian, and Jew. (Since Allport wrote, of course, African-American and black have largely displace Negro, and Orientals are rarely called "yellow.") The last part of this questions invites students to consider that such words exist for the sole purpose of expressing prejudice; when prejudice recedes, the words fall out of use.

5. Though the label _communist_ is no longer used as
frequently as it was in the 1950s to designate a scapegoat
in American society, it is still commonly employed to designate a perceived threat in the rest of the world. Thus
rebels in southeast Asia, Central America, and Africa are
often termed "communist" rather than nationalist, though
their politics have little or nothing in common.
6. When an individual emphatically rejects designation
by a particular label on the basis of the word's associations rather than its accuracy, he or she is displaying
symbol phobia (32). In paragraph 34 Allport explains verbal
realism: "When symbols provoke strong emotions they are
sometimes regarded no longer as symbols, but as actual
things." Thus many women who espouse complete equality for
women will refuse to be called "feminists" or "women's
liberationists," and those who argue about whether or not
abortion should be legal prefer to be labelled "pro-choice"
and "pro-life" rather than pro-abortion and anti-abortion.

Writing Topics (p. 445)

1. This exploration begins as an exercise in classification; the students are to define themselves in terms of
general attributes they share with some people but not with
others. But beyond this, the question asks them to consider
the relation between the way they see themselves and what
they believe strangers (responding to what Allport calls
"labels of primary potency") would think of them. Finally,
the students are asked to consider how Allport's "emotionally toned labels" have impinged on their lives. African-
American, Jewish, and other minority students will doubtless
have stories to tell, but so may others: the studious one
who was called a grind or an egghead, for example.
2. This question calls for some library research.
Since the issue of labels almost inevitably involves
prejudice, students should begin their search with sources
classified under the subject heading Prejudices and Antipa-
thies (this is where Allport's The Nature of Prejudice is
catalogued) and possibly move from there to more specialized
subject headings: Feminism, for example, if they are doing
research on women, or Negroes--Race Identity (through 1976)
and Blacks--Race Identity (since 1976--this change itself is
an example of the phenomenon) for African-Americans.

NEITHER WASP NOR JEW NOR BLACK

Michael Novak

Questions for Study and Discussion (p. 453)

1. There are no examples of feelings of "delight," in
Novak's essay, only feelings of being "blocked at every
turn," considered outside the "intellectual mainstream," and

feeling the country "did not belong to him."

2. Novak's remarks in paragraphs 19 and 20 reveal his and his family's conservative attitudes about sex. In paragraph 11 he is advised to "marry a Slovak girl" which, whether it is viewed as a means of maintaining the status quo or of not "muddying the waters," is also considered a conservative attitude. Novak's philosophy comes through as much in his diction as in his choice of examples. For example, Novak puts a negative spin on the word <u>intellectuals</u>, making them the heavies in a war against the "ethnics."

3. Novak mentions the following sub-groups in his essay: Irish Catholics, Lithuanians, Germans, Lebanese, English Catholics, PIGS, Anglo-Saxons, Christians, Jews, African-Americans, Chicanos and Indians. Many of these belong to "the workingmen of the nation," and do not share in the sense of belonging that Anglo-Saxons do. This is because Anglo-Saxons, English Catholics and Jews are "less inferior" than other ethnic groups, according to Novak. Novak distinguishes Slavs from other oppressed groups whose oppression is more visible and therefore evokes more sympathy.

4. Novak's thesis is that Americans do not welcome ethnics. Although Americans pride themselves on living in "a melting pot," the disparate "ingredients" are still distinguishable.

5. "Americans" are to blame for the following: Novak's feeling uneasy when he said his name, movie stars' changing their names to less European-sounding names, a failure of history classes to put ethnics in touch with their roots, and for ethnics' apologizing for food that smelled too strong for Anglo-Saxon noses. By these means Novak was denied some of the basics in order to "belong." These examples contribute to the charged tone of Novak's essay which nevertheless had elements of truth in it. How many of us have witnessed members of nationalities who do not accept tradition that is not their own, who poke fun at names that sound "too ethnic," and food that smells too European?

6. Novak reminds the reader that he has been oppressed, just as African-Americans have. However, he feels society sympathizes with oppression of African-Americans more than other racial and ethnic groups perhaps because that oppression is rooted in slavery--the cruelest oppression of all--and perhaps because the African-American struggle has been a visible part of our history for the last thirty years.

7. <u>Ethnic</u>, as Novak defines it, connotes anyone belonging to any cultural background other than the establishment groups such as White Anglo-Saxon Protestants. The dictionary definition defines <u>ethnic</u> as a "member or a minority group who retains the customs, language, or social views of his group." Novak's use of the word <u>ethnic</u> implies, as the dictionary does not, an inferior position. Although his tone is self-pitying, his point is valid.

8. No doubt Novak intends for his audience anyone who has not suffered as much as he has, which by his account would seem to be anyone who isn't Slavic. Witness his inclusion of virtually every other population group in the States among those who are the oppressors--"America, the America of the Anglo-Saxons and yes, in the arts, the Jews," "I was made to feel a slight uneasiness when I said my name," "Nowhere in my schooling do I recall any attempt to put me in touch with my own history," "power elite" that runs America (Ivy Leaguers), "keenly felt the absence of [that] sympathy for PIGS," terming others unlike him as "intellectuals."

Writing Topics (p. 454)

1. As a prewriting activity for this assignment you may encourage students to review the works of others who are very outspoken about their cause, and of activists such as Martin Luther King, Jr., who do more than just write about what they believe.
2. You may want to remind students that for this essay diction should be chosen carefully so as to have the maximum effect on their particular audience. The students can review the entry in the Glossary for DICTION.

ONE SMALL STEP FOR GENKIND

Casey Miller and Kate Swift

Questions for Study and Discussion (p. 465)

1. The authors' thesis appears in paragraph 3: " . . . our language, like the culture it reflects, is male oriented."
2. By defining everyone as male, as in the examples they cite--"If a man can walk 10 miles in two hours," "the man in the street," and "the man on the move"--Miller and Swift believe the English language assumes "that unless otherwise identified, people in general . . . are men," and this "semantic mechanism operates to keep women invisible" (4).
3. Miller and Swift provide a wide range of information to support their assertion that language works to keep women in "their place." A few of the more prominent examples are: 1) In education--they discuss the "reconstructed realities of American history" (8), and the dubious applications of definitions according to sexist male and female connotations; 2) In the media--they analyze how newspapers often identify a newsmaker as female when they would not do so for a man, and they reveal the specialized vocabulary often used to refer to females; 3) In religion--they examine how the Judeo-Christian mythology is the result of a patriarchal society and so the language of those myths

excludes or demeans women, and has led to an almost exclusively male ministry; and 4) In government--they take issue with the wording of the Constitution because it uses "he" only in describing the qualifications for government positions. There are many more examples students may cite. They may also identify ones from their own experiences or observations.

4. According to the authors, sexist language is that which is "almost impossible to use . . . without invoking cultural stereotypes." They cite the examples of "masculine" and "feminine," explaining that when people use these words "they almost always end up making assumptions that have nothing to do with innate differences between the sexes" (12).

5. The authors' discussion of the word "tomboy" illustrates the "subtle disparagement of females and corresponding approbation of males wrapped up in many English words" (17). For a girl who likes sports, or enjoys the outdoors, or is assertive, the label "tomboy" defines her "in terms of something she is not--a boy," and therefore "undermines her sense of identity: it says she is unnatural" (17).

6. Miller and Swift believe it is very important to eliminate the automatic use of <u>he</u>, <u>his</u>, and <u>him</u> because such language constructs "a reality in which women are ignored" and denied "recognition as people" (42). This ultimately leads to women "having grown up with a language that tells them they are at the same time men and not men," and rouses psychic doubts, "not of their sexual identity but of their human identity" (44). Students' responses to this analysis may vary, and can serve as the basis for class discussion of the gender problems created by the third person singular pronouns.

7. The examples and quotations are crucial to this essay's success because it is only by providing concrete evidence of sexist language "in action" that the authors will be able to convince readers that it is a real problem. In responding to this question students should consider what effect the essay would have on them if the examples or quotations or both were removed.

8. The authors' tone in this essay is reasonable yet quite firm in its opposition to the current state of male-oriented language. Their selections in diction that convey this firmness include the following:

"operates to keep women <u>invisible</u>" (4)

"unintentional <u>skewings</u>" (9)

"Masculine and feminine, however, are as <u>sexist as any words can be</u>" (12)

"<u>subtle disparagement</u> of females" (17)

"<u>invidious</u> comparisons and <u>stereotypes</u>" (18)

"conventions of the news media add <u>insult to injury</u>" (20)

"Attitudes of <u>ridicule, contempt and disgust</u> toward female sexuality" (25)

"An <u>entire</u> mythology has grown from this <u>biological misunderstanding</u>" (29)

"<u>male-dominated</u> culture" (30)

"When language <u>oppresses</u>, it does so by <u>any means that disparage and belittle</u>" (36)

"<u>Nowhere</u> are women rendered <u>more invisible</u>" (40)

"a reality in which women are <u>ignored</u>"

Miller and Swift maintain a sense of reasonableness, despite the strong phrases cited above, by presenting and explaining appropriate examples that support the claims expressed through such emphatic diction.

9.   The title of this essay is a reference to the famous words Neil Armstrong spoke as he first stepped on the moon--"This is one small step for man, one giant leap for mankind." By changing "mankind" to "genkind" the authors are putting into practice their belief that we need to make conscious attempts at eliminating sexual bias from our language. They explain the particular appropriateness of "genkind" as a substitute for "mankind" in the final paragraph.

<u>Writing Topics (p. 465)</u>

1.   Students will no doubt find it helpful to discuss this topic in class before they begin writing. To stimulate such discussion you can bring in sample newspapers or magazines and have students look through them, identifying examples of language that demonstrates a male-oriented bias. After they have located a few, discuss what effect these examples might have on readers' attitudes toward women. By looking at specific cases of male-oriented language and discussing their importance and, perhaps, their application to students' own lives, students may find it easier to formulate opinions about the power language has in shaping society's attitudes.
2.   As a prewriting activity for this topic you can go back and evaluate exactly how Miller and Swift have incorporated their beliefs about language into the writing of their essay. Try to locate examples that show a deliberate attempt to eliminate sexist language. Have students analyze one or two other essays or articles in a magazine or local newspaper for sexist language. If students find objectionable language, ask them how they might rewrite the passage

to eliminate the sexism. This type of analysis and discussion may help students recognize things they as users of language can do to bring about change and improve the lot of women in this country.

3. It may be interesting to share the results of this assignment, since students may be surprised by the feelings others hold in regard to particular obscenities, or by the associations sometimes attached to them, as in Miller's and Swift's suggestion of the savagery of rape. As a follow-up, then, you can have students do a short writing exercise in which they describe how the variety of responses to sexual obscenities has affected their own attitudes toward them.

4. As a prewriting activity for this topic you can elicit examples from students' own experiences where they have recognized that problems with sexist language still remain. Females, in particular, may have observations to offer on how they have felt "left out" by male-oriented language. Males, though, may have insights to share on how their language often coerces them into making sexually biased statements, even against their inclinations not to do so, because they are not presently aware of suitable alternatives. Discussion of these issues may provide more information from which students can draw conclusions about whether we have reason to be optimistic or pessimistic about the future.

SEXISM AND LANGUAGE

Alleen Pace Nilsen

Questions for Study and Discussion (p. 472)

1. Nilsen explicitly states that our language is an indicator of our values, values which glorify men and disdain women.

2. Through our job titles, product names, and labels we glorify men. Nilsen uses numerous examples to strengthen her point.

3. Nilsen's opinions are witty and demonstrate that she has a sound understanding of how language works. In paragraph 7, for example, she gives a probable reason for the "negative connotation of old age in women." She supports her generalizations with multiple examples. Her evidence is thorough, enlightening, and generally convincing.

4. Our language makes men strong and wise and renders women beautiful yet passive.

5. The machine age has changed the status of man's strength. As he has relinquished tasks to machines, not only has his strength increasingly paled relative to that of the machines, it has inevitably declined in comparison to the strength of women.

6. Nilsen's tone is reasonable, logical, and good-natured. Nilsen maintains this tone through careful description and by drawing conclusions only after all the evidence has been presented. Her witty observations are a good-natured invitation to share in Nilsen's delight in the study of our language.

7. In paragraph 17, Nilsen cites the work of James Ney on anti-male biases in English. Ney concludes that if "English speakers want to call a man something bad, there seems to be a large vocabulary available to them but if they want to use a term which is good to describe a male, there is a small vocabulary available. The reverse is true for women." While Nilsen acknowledges the anti-male bias in English, she seems to believe that it doesn't begin to measure up to the anti-female bias she has found. She argues that our positive and negative feelings about both males and females are directly related to the roles these people play. Her line of argument is both reasonable and convincing.

Writing Topics (p. 472)

1. The list of questions posed offers a good focus for class discussion of the subtle sexism that exists in language. Through such a discussion students may come to recognize elements of sexism or sexist assumptions in their own use of language, which they can shape into their own essays.

2. To help students get started on this assignment you may want to conduct a brainstorming session in which they generate examples of fad words, such as computer terms or social terms. Are these similar to Nilsen's words? Do these words die completely? Are any expressions so inappropriate that they have a short life span?

KING OF THE BINGO GAME

Ralph Ellison

Questions for Study and Discussion (p. 481)

1. It is not apparent that the protagonist is an African-American until well into the story when he is on stage. By then the reader has also had enough clues to know that the protagonist is poor and hungry and that his wife or girlfriend is very sick with an unnamed illness. It is his concern for her that has brought him again and again to the movie hall to try to win money. Some students say that after reading the headnote on Ellison and The Invisible Man and seeing the references to "folks down South" and "white people laughing," they suspected that the protagonist was African-American.

2. The protagonist is not mad; he is desperate, a

condition sometimes indistinguishable from madness. The reader is made to feel this sense of desperation, the sense that this is his very last chance to do something for the woman he loves.

3. Ellison heightens our awareness of the protagonist's sense of alienation by including not only the facts of his poverty, but by including his sense of separation from his native environment. He is from the South, a hard place but at least a familiar one. Now he has been thrown into the vast unknown of the North, a place he no doubt felt would be a Mecca but is instead just a different kind of hell. although he is surrounded by fellow African-Americans in the audience, he is still uncomfortable, the more so because the bingo master delights in humiliating contestants. He talks to himself, keeps his own company, shunning those who, although they are probably very much like him, seem to him to be less unlucky.

4. The dollar amount seems pitifully low, but evidently is enough for the hero's needs. The value of the dollar, the contrasts between the North and the South, and the silent movie with musical accompaniment indicate that this is set in the 1930s.

5. The protagonist sees the wheel as controlling his destiny so he grabs it and holds on as long as he can, until they physically drag him out. The game and his defeat are a powerful metaphor for the desperation and victimization of the African-American man. The use of the phrase "King of Bingo" is also a metaphor--a bleak, sad, unfilled wish for power. At the end of the story the author uses irony to make his point that the protagonist was in some way responsible for his own undoing at the moment of victory. Students will also find examples of the author's use of simile in the story.

6. Our hero views the wheel as his ultimate destiny and he is afraid to let go of it, to lose control. His reference to himself as the "King of Bingo" is a desperate wish for power and luck.

7. The irony of the ending of the story is that the man was denied victory at the last moment, not by bad luck, but because he was too afraid to allow it to happen.

Writing Topics (p. 482)

1. Students may be reminded that a metaphor is an implied comparison rather than an explicit one as with a simile. You may also refer students to the entry in the Glossary at the back of the book for FIGURES OF SPEECH. Students may wish to experiment with metonymy and synecdoche for this assignment.

2. This is a good assignment to familiarize students with the various reference tools in the library. Students may find reference to dance marathons in the periodical catalog as well as history books of the era.

POLITICS AND THE ENGLISH LANGUAGE

George Orwell

Questions for Study and Discussion (p. 494)

1. As Orwell has it, bad politics--the unthinking reiteration of the party line, the defense of the indefensible, and the like--makes for foggy and stale language. Most would agree. But he goes on to argue that such language in turn can be an obstacle to honesty and sincerity in politics. (See paragraph 2.)

2. Orwell defines dying metaphors (5), operators or verbal false limbs (6), pretentious diction (7), and meaningless words (8), all of them hackneyed, prefabricated devices which substitute for actual thinking. He explains each by providing numerous common examples.

3. Prefabricated houses are not chosen or built because they reflect the buyer's taste. They are look-alike, mass-produced structures which have no individuality. Similarly prefabricated phrases are "long strips of words which have been already set in order by someone else" (11) and release one from the responsibility of choosing words which express one's exact meaning. In both the prefabricated houses and prefabricated language, quality is sacrificed for convenience and economy of effort.

4. Students should be asked to consider exactly what is being compared to what in each case, then to analyze why Orwell thought each particular comparison appropriate to its context.

> a. "A huge dump of worn-out metaphors" suggests trash heap of objects that were once useful but no longer work--an obviously appropriate figure of speech, which also implies that those who use such metaphors are picking over the trash and garbage of language.
> b. Used tea leaves, again, are garbage, and the figure of speech suggests that "stale" phrases "choke" off the flow of communication just as the leaves choke off the flow of water out of the sink.
> c. Euphemism, of which Orwell considers the inflated style an example, is meant to soften the impact of sharp, unpleasant truths. Snow, of course, softens the sharp outlines of objects. And both euphemism and snow succeed in "covering up the details."
> d. Both the politician and the cuttlefish (or squid) are to be seen as escaping from danger and covering their retreats. The comparison is

the more amusing because both may use ink,
though ejecting it from different orifices.

   e. Cavalry horses are so thoroughly trained that
   they recognize and obey bugle calls as a conditioned reflex. Orwell's simile is appropriate
   because it suggests that the "familiar dreary
   pattern" of the pamphleteer's words is absolutely rigid and unvarying, like a military
   formation, and also that the number of patterns
   available to that writer, like the number of
   bugle calls used by an army, is extremely
   limited.

   5. Orwell's essay contains remarkably few stale or
vague phrases. In paragraph 1, "It is generally assumed,"
"so the argument runs," and "it follows that" are overly
familiar devices. In paragraph 2 Orwell uses an unwarranted
construction: "It is clear that." In fact, Orwell frequently begins his sentences with the impersonal construction "it is," as for example in paragraph 12--"It is broadly
true that" and "It will generally be found"--and this is a
rather wordy way to get a sentence going. "Pad" in paragraph 6 is a metaphor which he must often have seen in
print. But these lapses are few and minor, and his acknowl-
edgment has the effect of disarming readers and convincing
them that he is modest, reasonable, and aware of the difficulty of avoiding ready-made constructions.

   6. Orwell's final rule underlines a central point:
that good writing emphasizes meaning, not obedience to any
set of rules, even his own. As he says in paragraph 18, his
point "has nothing to do with correct grammar and syntax,
which are of no importance as long as one makes one's meaning clear. . . . What is above all needed is to let the
meaning choose the word, and not the other way about."

Writing Topics (p. 495)

   1. Situations such as this topic outline come up in
most people's daily lives, and they are generally dealt with
through white lies (or lies that are not so white). Handling such situations in an honest way, yet still avoiding a
premature or damaging answer, is problematic because it
usually reveals that one is holding something back. This
issue in practical ethics is surprisingly knotty, as is
suggested by Sissela Bok's Lying: Moral Choice in Public
and Private Life (1978).

   2. Students should have no difficulty locating examples
in the newspaper, especially in the New York Times, which
regularly prints political speeches in their entirety. The
Iran-Contra or the savings-and-loan hearings revealed many
such abuses of language.

   3. The purpose of Newspeak was to manipulate truth, to
distort history, and to control the minds of its users.
Thus, Newspeak is a fictionalized extension of the tenden-
cies toward manipulative language that Orwell warned against

in "Politics and the English Language." Interestingly, the people of <u>1984</u> began using Newspeak voluntarily and more and more frequently, pushing ahead its projected timetable as the standard language of Oceania.

PROPAGANDA: HOW NOT TO BE BAMBOOZLED

Donna Woolfolk Cross

<u>Questions for Study and Discussion (p. 506)</u>

    1. According to Cross, the propagandist can influence our thinking by "appealing to our emotions, distracting our attention, misleading us with logic that may appear to be reasonable but is in fact faulty and deceiving" (46), and using testimonials or endorsements from public figures who, in effect, we let "make our decisions for us" (50).
    2. The testimonial which "consists in having some loved or respected person give a statement of support (testimonial) for a given product or idea" (47) is the device most often used by propagandists. Advertising abounds with examples of testimonials: for example, model Linda Evangelista endorsing a brand of make-up, or retired professional athletes praising a particular beer. Politicians also use endorsements, whether from other politicians or from television and movie actors or even from carefully selected "ordinary" citizens.
    3. Cross first defines the device, then proceeds by giving at least two examples, one involving "Senator Yakalot." In her closing paragraph for each section she explains the device's intent and tells us how to defend ourselves against it and think for ourselves. Cross seems to organize her devices of propaganda by beginning with the most obvious techniques (name calling, glittering generalities) and moving to the more "insidious," easily overlooked ones.
    4. Cross attributes the familiar propagandistic phrases to Senator Yakalot (<u>yak</u> is slang for <u>talk</u>), a fictitious politician who stands for all the real politicians who have used these demagogic tactics.
    5. Cross compares people who support a popular cause with lemmings, who are driven by instinct to rush into deep water and drown themselves. The analogy is apt because both the lemmings and the masses of people are operating by sheer instinct and not by reason—and, often, against their own best interests. The analogy is not altogether accurate, however, since lemmings are genetically compelled to drown themselves, while people can decide to hold back from the crowd.

1. Students may use fund-raising literature and advertising by UNICEF, the American Cancer Society, and overseas relief organizations as examples. Undoubtedly, such propaganda appeals to people's emotions rather than to their reason and seeks to make them feel strongly about a cause, perhaps overlooking legitimate issues such as how much of their money is spent not only helping people but on paying the fund-raisers. However, except perhaps among tax accountants, the decision to give is often unselfish and emotional, and it is hard to imagine an effective charitable campaign that is not mainly emotional in appeal.

2. Propaganda is not only difficult to avoid using in persuasion but often has considerably more "crowd appeal" than does logical argument. Glittering generalities, ad hominem arguments, begging the question, and false dilemmas are particularly common pitfalls. Students who think themselves above using propaganda will find this an enlightening exercise--and all will find it an essential one as a preparation for college work.

THE RONALD REAGAN BASIC 1984 CAMPAIGN SPEECH

The New York Times

Questions for Study and Discussion (p. 512)

1. Reagan's definition of patriotism as a recognition that one's country is a decent place to live and is a force for good in the world conforms closely to the dictionary definition of the word, i.e. a love of one's country. However, some students will argue that love of country does not imply, "my country right or wrong," as Reagan's definition does. They will further argue that a proud citizenry has the right to question the policies of his country without being labeled "unpatriotic."

2. The question some students will ask is "freer than what?" In order to understand Reagan's use of the word "freer," we have to understand Reagan's concept of the word "free."

3. Reagan was referring to the Carter administration. The word "they" connotes a formless, faceless reality and in this case is uttered in a slightly mocking tone. It permits the audience to nod assent, to agree with the speaker that the faults of the "they" are so well-known that "they" don't even have to be identified by name. It allows the speaker to imply, "I don't have to call you by name, we all know who you are."

4. Most college students know that statistics can be used to "prove" almost anything. For example, in order to evaluate the relative accuracy of Reagan's statement that six million new jobs were "created" during the first four

years of his administration, a student would also have to know how many jobs were "lost." Reagan alludes to reductions in federal spending (11), however, he does not say how those reductions may have resulted in increased state spending. In the matter of interest rates, some economists maintain that these rates are slow to react to policies and that each administration bears the gift or the burden of the policies of the previous administration. So in order to answer the question of who can legitimately take credit for improvements, a student needs a sophisticated and broad-based understanding of the various factors that influence change and economics. For the most part, presidents are made or broken on the popular perception of the truth of their claims.

5. By reminding his listeners that he was once, and still considers himself, a member of the Democratic Party, Reagan is bridging the gap that many Democrats would normally feel exist between themselves and a Republican presidential candidate. In effect, Reagan is suggesting to the voters in his audience that he shares their ideology.

6. "There's a feeling of patriotism in our land. . . . And I don't know about you but I'm tired of hearing people run her down" (1).

"For them to introduce that blueprint for bondage in Philadelphia . . . was a betrayal of the American people" (12). "They see an America where every day is April 15th, tax day. We see an America where every day is the Fourth of July" (15).

"I am telling you that what I felt was that the leadership of the Democratic Party had left me and millions of patriotic Democrats in this country who believed in freedom" (28).

7. Reagan uses simple phrasing and avoids a fancy vocabulary, which make it easy to follow his speech. He also asks the members of his audience questions in an almost evangelical style that elicits an energetic response and draws them into his thinking. Another aspect of this style is his ability to fire up a crowd with frequent reference to America's best image of itself as a patriotic, decent place to live.

Writing Topics (p. 512)

1. A class discussion of Reagan's speeches will allow students to exchange ideas and insights as to the key elements of his style. It might be helpful to assign the speeches of other presidents also known for their powerful rhetoric in order that students may contrast with Reagan's speeches, the ways in which they grab listener attention.

Point out to students that in answering the several questions presented in this Writing Topic, they will have formed an outline for their final essay.

2. Refer students to works dealing with the McCarthy Era of the fifties, during which a special committee of the

110

United States Senate, headed by Senator Joseph McCarthy, accused thousands of people of being "card-carrying members of the communist party." Suggest to students that they might want to consider which elements of "McCarthyism," if any, were present in Bush's denouncement of Dukakis.

NAMING OF PARTS

Henry Reed

Questions for Study and Discussion (p. 514)

1. In this poem, an instructor is talking to a class about the different parts of a gun.
2. By placing the action of the poem in a garden, the author is able to contrast the warm beauty and innocence of nature with the cold, deliberateness of war.
3. The language of the gun is hard and steely. The language of the garden is soft and yielding.
4. Besides the students' not having their "piling swivel," we have not got the "silent, eloquent gestures" and the "point of balance" found in nature.
5. Reed uses repetition to create a military-like chant and to drum home his point.
6. Reed seems to be saying that nature fulfills her promise gently and without connivance, while war requires a sharp edge and calculating thinking.

Writing Topics (p. 514)

1. As a prewriting activity for this assignment it may be helpful to have students offer their interpretations of these two phrases. This may help students organize their thoughts and focus on their ideas before writing their essays.
2. It may be helpful to have students read the selection by Leo Cawley entitled "Refighting the War: Why the Movies are in Vietnam." This will give students one point of view on how war is depicted for us.

HARRISON BERGERON

Kurt Vonnegut, Jr.

Questions for Study and Discussion (p. 520)

1. When students take a close look at the story they will be surprised at how little the world it depicts differs from the world of today. For example, people then talk much as they do today, they still watch television, ballet still exists as does canned beer, and Diana Moon Glampers arms herself with a double-barreled ten-gauge shotgun. The only

difference is that in 2081 equality of ability has been imposed by handicapping the talented. Vonnegut's intention is clearly to focus the reader's attention wholly on the theme of his story--total equality. Had he created a more futuristic world, he would have run the risk of diverting the reader's attention from that theme.

2.   George refers to the competitive past as the "dark ages" because he believes that the present (2081) is a more enlightened and civilized time. Handicapping eliminates the ability to excel and thus makes competition pointless if not impossible. In this world any exceptional and underhandi-capped person (like Harrison) is dangerous because the society of 2081 would "fall all apart" (33)--or, as nearly happens, because such a person might try to become an abso-lute ruler.

3.   Some specific handicaps that people have to wear are sashweights, bags of birdshot, masks and clown noses, and receivers so that they could be "buzzed" with assorted noises to prevent the possibility of connected thought. These handicaps are essentially comical and suggest the work of a fertile but odd imagination. That the people of 2081 accept such indignities reveals how conditioned and unthink-ing they have become.

4.   One reason that Vonnegut made Harrison Bergeron a fourteen-year-old boy is to show us a character whose mind and body are still developing and whose handicaps therefore need constant monitoring. His first appearance in paragraph 54 suggests something of the child, but otherwise there is little that is childish about him--he is, after all, excep-tional.

5.   Shifting to fantasy at this point in the story allows Vonnegut to create an extreme contrast with the flat, equalized world he has been describing up to this point. (And perhaps, after all, by 2081 an exceptional human being would have been able to do what Harrison does.) A less fantastic climax might have been more believable, but then the story is not meant to be believable; it is a parable on the theme of equality.

6.   Diana Moon Glampers, as the person who assigns handicaps and enforces them, is the true ruler of 2081 society. Her job requires careful assessments of everyone's ability and the measured handicapping of each person to achieve a balanced equality, and when the system is threat-ened she takes direct, calculated, effective action. Hazel thinks, in paragraph 18, that she'd "make a good Handicapper General," but immediately reveals that she is too soft-hearted and probably too dull-witted for the job. It's notable that the handicaps Diana Moon Glampers imposes are comical and reductive not only of capability but of dignity, and also that she is evidently empowered to kill violators of the handicapping laws without a trial.

7.   If all men are created equal, as the Declaration of Independence asserts, they are certainly not created aver-age. Equality, as defended in American tradition and law,

is a matter of equal standing before the law and equal opportunity to try to succeed--not of equal talent, or equal success regardless of talent. In Vonnegut's story the social ideal is not equality but the average, which requires that the above-average be brought down and the below-average (like the radio announcer in paragraphs 37-38) be elevated to positions they are ill-equipped to fill.

Writing Topics (p. 521)

1. Exploring American attitudes toward exceptional people can be enlightening. School children tend to admire athletically gifted classmates rather than the brainy ones, and many carry that prejudice into adult life--evidently we would rather feel relatively clumsy than relatively stupid. Political leaders attract not only enthusiastic followers but assassins; the very rich excite curiosity, envy, and admiration simply because of their wealth. The attitude Vonnegut satirizes in "Harrison Bergeron," that of wanting to bring exceptional people down to one's level (though not, of course, to reduce oneself to a still lower level!), has long appealed to those who think it particularly democratic, and may explain the success of some very mediocre people in public life. But of course too much respect for the exceptional person, especially the exceptional politician, can lead to dictatorship and disaster, as in Germany in the 1930s.

2. Those who support or indeed oppose the various programs mentioned here may not have thought of them in quite the terms we pose. Even if one favors affirmative action on the grounds of fairness, for example, it may mean that one's education, or one's open heart surgery, is being conducted by a less qualified and able person than would otherwise have been the case.

3. Both Vonnegut and Auden are satirizing imaginary societies that are much like our own and that take the ordinary man as the norm. In both works the society values conformity highly and places no value on individuality or on the individual's feelings and aspirations. In Auden's poem, however, the average, "unknown citizen" is arrived at by statistical means, whereas in "Harrison Bergeron" average citizens are created through handicapping.

Culture

HOW WE LISTEN

Aaron Copland

Questions for Study and Discussion (p. 530)

　　1.　Refer to paragraph 11 where Copland explains that
Beethoven is difficult to interpret, whereas Tchaikovsky is
easy to interpret because his theme is always the same (and
is, therefore, dull).　Since Tchaikovsky is easier to interpret, "musical novices" who judge music by its interpreta-
bility may consider him a better composer.
　　2.　On the first plane the listener absorbs the music.
On the second plane the listener interprets the music.　On
the third plane the listener is conscious of the actual
movement of the notes.　Each successive plane requires more
involvement from the listener.　Copland makes these distinctions clear to his reader by explaining when these instances
would occur.
　　3.　Copland compares listening to music to watching a
play.　Absorbing the actors and scenery is similar to awareness on the sensuous plane.　Reacting emotionally to them is
similar to awareness on the expressive plane.　Understanding
the plot and its development is similar to awareness on the
musical plane.　Copland's explanations were made infinitely
clearer by the use of this comparison.
　　4.　Music does not necessarily have the same meaning
for all listeners.　This lends to wider appreciation because
different people can find meaning of their own.　Each piece
can also have different meanings throughout the composition.
For instance, a musical composition can render a progression
of emotions, a span of time or a change of seasons.
　　5.　"Tone color" is different instruments playing the
same note, yet by virtue of their differences rendering a
different "color" to the note.
　　6.　Copland explains that even though the listener
cannot attach a singular meaning to a piece of music, it
does not mean the listener has not understood the whole
meaning of the music.
　　7.　Copland is writing for a general readership as
evidenced by his simple explanation of the planes and his
use of analogy at the end.　However, a definition of "tone
colors" would help the reader.　Most students, whether they
are musicians or not, should be able to relate to and com-
prehend his discussions of Beethoven and Tchaikovsky.

1. It may be interesting for you to get a selection from the library and play it in class. After the selection has ended you may facilitate a discussion about the three planes relative to that piece of music and the students' experience listening to it.

2. Again, you may want to videotape an act from "A Midsummer Night's Dream" or another comedy so students can determine their feelings about Shakespeare, especially if they have never been exposed to his work. This can help students focus on their own thoughts to organize their essays.

GEORGIA O'KEEFFE

Joan Didion

Questions for Study and Discussion (p. 534)

1. Didion explains that the poem or painting does not always reflect the thoughts and emotions of the artist as the audience interprets them. For example, a painter need not be sad to paint a blue-tone picture.

2. O'Keeffe paints from the heart, according to Didion. "She did not much care" how Impressionists "did" trees; O'Keeffe drew trees as she saw them. This sentiment can be taken to mean that the greatest value of classwork for someone like O'Keeffe is solely as a means of improving technique.

3. The attitude that only men will truly survive as artists while women will teach or model, and that the "true" artist must be schooled and classified, left its impression even among artists. However, O'Keeffe always knew who she was and stood armed and ready to battle those who suppressed her as a woman and an artist.

4. Didion describes O'Keeffe in the following ways: "beautiful face," "hard woman," "neither 'crusty' nor eccentric," "straight shooter," "clean of received wisdom," "open to what she sees," "astonishingly aggressive." Didion brings her daughter to a viewing of O'Keeffe's work thereby passing on her admiration of the artist to her daughter. Didion describes the tone others use to describe O'Keeffe as "condescending romance." If Didion agreed with this assessment she probably would have not chosen to express it this way. Didion refers to O'Keeffe as a "successful guerrilla." Therefore, Didion seems to admire O'Keeffe as a successful, hard-working woman.

5. Didion says that it is basic to assume that "style is character." If Didion believed this to be true, she probably would not describe it as an assumption.

1. Students may want to consider the fact that many authors were not accepted when their writing was first presented. Some authors could not get published and some works were distributed more after the author died. Students may research this and discern why authors are not accepted at first by reviewing biographies of older authors.

2. As a prewriting activity you may have the class analyze Didion's style to find out what makes it distinct, by examining her use of anecdote, adjective, or metaphor. This may help students to recognize strategy and focus their thoughts to organize their essays.

MODERN ART

Katherine Kuh

Questions for Study and Discussion (p. 539)

1. Kuh is referring to the fragmentation of art.

2. Experiments with optical color laws, natural and artificial light, microscopes, atom bombs, and X-ray machines have all changed the way we think about the world and ourselves. As a result the artist has a wider and more varied spectrum of views and topics to draw upon and new ways in which to present them. Freud's psychology has also influenced art. However, while Kuh explains that computer graphics have brought a new dimension to art, she does not discuss the public's perception of it.

3. Impressionism took art outdoors with color broken into minute areas. Expressionism presented pitted surfaces with unpredictable colors. Cubism showed all sides of an object by painting part of it transparently, while the Italian Futurists of the period were showing the object's path of motion. Surrealism showed an object from different angles at the same time. Abstract Impressionism presented harsh brush strokes. It is sometimes difficult to understand the terms Kuh uses to distinguish the different eras in art, and her points are not always clearly drawn. It might have helped if she had mentioned examples of artworks from the different eras that students are familiar with.

4. Kuh begins her essay by discussing how "break up" has become increasingly more incorporated into art. She demonstrates her point using a chronology of art eras. Kuh then presents a chronology of the scientific and psychological influences on art. While her chronologies are easy enough to follow, the art novice may find her terminology an obstacle.

5. Kuh implies that art's "break up" is the symbolization of the way science has forced us to see the world through a fractured lens.

116

1.   Students should be reminded of the role examples can play in establishing the differences and changes in art forms over the years. It is important that their reader "sees" the students' ideas in this essay.

2.   Before assigning this topic it may be fun to hand out an in class "pseudo" assignment in which you tell the students exactly what they must write about. Once the papers are handed in you can "grade" them based on standards that you have determined but not told the students, such as points off for not leaving three spaces blank at the top of the page, or points off for students who do not dot "i"s or write in cursive. This will give students the experience of being critiqued based on standards that oppose their own.

ON ESSAYS

Edward Hoagland

Questions for Study and Discussion (p. 543)

1.   Hoagland explains that stories are the root of art. He explains that story telling was the first art form and from it came poems, songs, and drawings to depict a story. He adds that behind every piece of art there is also a story.

2.   Hoagland feels that there are two ends on a person's continuum. On one end is what you are, the real you. On the other end is what you think, the ideal you. Although a person may write about environmental ideals, the writer may not be a true environmentalist. Such an essay would be far to the left of the "real" end of the continuum.

3.   Hoagland uses the properties of fur and cotton to describe the differences between a personal essay and a magazine article. He describes the essay as rough and outstanding because it carries the style of the writer. The article, however, is stripped of style to cohere with the rest of the magazine. While Hoagland's point is clearly stately, it could have been said more simply.

4.   Hoagland feels that shaving the truth in an essay is justifiable except when making an argument. In that case it is not fair to the reader to base an argument on near lies. However, to make an essay interesting, shaving the truth does not hurt the reader.

5.   Hoagland compares the essay to several types of familiar writing. He weaves his discussion of these other types throughout his discussion of the essay in a way that is easy to follow.

6.   The novel can give the reader a full idea of a story and its characters, but the essay is flexible. The essay can change to "suit the times."

1. It may be helpful to review the works of a couple of these authors so that students can determine what traits of the author is revealed in their work. Students who have not taken many literature courses may benefit from biographies supplied by books such as <u>Literature: The Human Experience</u>, fifth edition, by Richard Abcarian and Marvin Klotz (St. Martin's Press, 1990).

2. As a prewriting activity you may have students define "essay" in class by writing the individual definitions or one definition that each student adds to on the board. This may help students clarify their own position before starting the assignment and understand the differences between an essay and the other types of writing that Hoagland discusses.

BULLCRIT

Richard Rosen

Questions for Study and Discussion (p. 551)

1. "Bullcrit" is the art of learning and theorizing about a subject from all but first-hand accounts. The implication of the word is that as much as we like to impress others with our commentaries and reviews, we are too intellectually lazy to actually read what we review.

2. It is still prestigious to own and to have read certain books. Authors remain in the limelight because they are reviewed, even if nobody reads them. An author can always aspire for the ultimate in the literary world--having his work turned into a screen play.

3. Rosen quotes Gore Vidal in paragraph 24 as saying, "It has always been true that in the United States the people who ought to read books write them." This quote states emphatically and cynically that even authors are not readers and their work proves it.

4. People sometimes lie to create an impression or maintain an image. However, if a person who weighs 250 pounds claims to weigh 150 pounds, no one is fooled. The predominant effect of such lies is to make the teller seem foolish.

5. Rosen is exploring the possibility that people read and review books to impress others. However, that desire implies a stake in the outcome. It is this stake that Rosen thinks will negate the objectivity of a review. The resolution is that the reader can usually tell very clearly where the reviewer is coming from especially after several such reviews. Then the risk is on the part of the reviewer where it belongs and the listener is no danger.

6. Our culture tolerates any form of entertainment that is visual. In other words, it tolerates anything that

does not require it to think or use its imagination. According to Rosen, Americans would rather wait for the movie.

Writing Topics (p. 552)

1.   The student may approach this assignment two ways.
They may write a narrative leading up to a time when they
tried to get away with being unprepared for an oral report
in anecdote form, or the students can contrast a time when
they were not prepared to a time when they were. In each
case it will be important for the students to express the
emotions they felt when they realized they did not know what
they were talking about.
2.   It may be helpful to discuss in class novels that
were made into motion pictures, such as "Jaws," "The Color
Purple," "Amityville Horror," "Love Story," and "Wuthering
Heights." For those who have read or seen these stories,
the emotional responses may be different between reading the
book and watching the movie.

Pop Culture

REFIGHTING THE WAR: WHY THE MOVIES ARE IN VIETNAM

Leo Cawley

Questions for Study and Discussion (p. 560)

1.   Cawley answers the questions he poses in paragraph
2 indirectly. In fact, Cawley's purpose in writing his
essay is to raise and respond to these vital questions.
2.   The bitterest dramas occurred after GIs came home
and had to face disinterest and accusations from family and
friends in addition to their own memory of what they had
done in Vietnam (7).
3.   Modern movies about Vietnam force Americans to face
their acts of cruelty toward defenseless Vietnamese civil-
ians.
4.   Hippies believed GIs were murderers in a senseless
war. The GIs saw themselves as the thankless defenders of
the Democratic way of life.
5.   Vietnam War movies, unlike WW II movies, show the
rise of "lesser loyalties," which replace a previous faith
in the government and an anticommunist bond among Americans.
These new loyalties have prevented a discussion of what
"really went on in Vietnam" according to Cawley and have
allowed the perpetuation of a series of myths about American
goodness.
6.   Many students (most of whom are only recently luck-
less adolescents themselves) will find this statement absurd
since if a generation is killed off at war, there is no
future for that country.

Writing Topics (p. 561)

1. As a prewriting topic, have students consider cover-ups on a personal, state, or national level. Do these cover-ups begin intentionally? Do the perpetrators eventually believe in the information they reveal as the truth? For example, use insurance salespersons: although they are salespeople, they are not known in the industry to be keen on policy exceptions, exclusions, and coverages. They make many promises when a client takes out a policy. These may not be informed promises, and the salespersons may really believe in what they pitch, especially if a mistake is never brought to their attention.

2. It may be helpful for students to try to determine why organizations withhold information. This can be done through a cause and effect analysis taking into account the different types of causes.

WHY WE CRAVE HORROR MOVIES

Stephen King

Questions for Study and Discussion (p. 564)

1. We go to horror movies to show that we are not afraid, to reestablish our feelings of being normal, and to have fun. Some people go to satisfy a morbid curiosity about how the horror will be effected, or because they are aficionados of the macabre.

2. King compares the thrills and chills of the roller coaster ride with the thrills and chills of the horror movie. Each propels you along, promising to reward your terror at the next turn; and each fulfills that promise . . . when you least expect it.

3. The horror movie maintains the status quo of the nature of good and evil and beauty and ugliness in our minds. It does not ask us to rework our values.

4. Society applauds love, friendship, loyalty, and kindness because they "maintain the status quo of civilization itself." King labels emotions that are mean and murderous as "anticivilization."

5. The sick joke and the horror movie both appeal "to all that is worst in us." Both unchain our basest, most immoral instincts.

6. King gives examples of strange behavior that occurs in all of us, moving from the innocence of people who talk to themselves to the potentially murderous "lyncher." His last line suggests, as Freud did, that a darker, more menacing creature lies in wait beneath the civilized exterior we present to the world.

7. King's tone is humorously menacing. He, like the horror movie he describes, likes to lead the viewer along and then, without warning, spring at him with a grisly

thought or a shocking idea. His first and final sentences are meant to bring the reader up short. In between, students will find numerous examples of his scary prose. For example, "if your insanity leads you to carve up women," "the potential lyncher is in almost all of us," "but if you deliberately slam the rotten little puke of a sister's fingers in the door, sanctions follow." King also goes so far as to repeat for us one of the more horrifying of the "sick" jokes.

Writing Topics (p. 565)

1. This assignment indirectly first asks the students to discern who King and his cohorts write for. You might conduct a discussion in which this is determined, or ask students to address this in their essays.
2. Students may approach this from the other side of the argument. For example, some students may never have seen a horror movie. These students may write an essay discussing why they have never seen a horror movie, and what their perceptions of these movies are.

MUSIC

Allan Bloom

Questions for Study and Discussion (p. 578)

1. Although music, literature, and art technically are available to everyone, it seems that the educated possess other advantages such as the money and the leisure time necessary to enjoy the arts.
2. According to Bloom, indignation describes an uneducated society's discomfort with things they do not understand. The paragraphs offering several instances of indignation support Bloom's thesis that society and individuals have violent feelings about music.
3. Bloom assumes that his young readers are familiar with Plato. Those unfamiliar with Plato's specific attitude toward music may find Bloom's references confusing.
4. "The lefts" are radicals and "the rights" are conservatives. These two groups can influence the industry by making consumers aware of what is going on from their point of view. For example, "the rights" want to label albums so consumers are aware of their "sex content," and "the lefts" monitor albums' "violence content."
5. Bloom feels rock music is more accessible than television, but many students will disagree. Long before children are exposed to radio and records, they are watching television.
6. In paragraph 16, Bloom claims that the size of the industry accounts for its respectability. "Respectability" in this instance refers to the fact that because of its

size, and power, the music industry must be taken seriously. The word "respectability" seems somewhat inappropriate since size does not necessarily denote quality.

<u>Writing Topics (p. 578)</u>

1. As a prewriting activity for this assignment you may want to hold an informal debate between those offended by the record labeling and those who see no harm in letting consumers know exactly what the song's lyrics are. This topic has received much news coverage in the past 3-5 years, so students should be able to locate appropriate articles in <u>The Readers' Guide to Periodical Literature</u>.

2. In order to facilitate ideas for this assignment, you may have students consider which are the "good" rock groups today. How many of these groups were active and/or popular before 1981 when MTV was not on television? You may also have the students consider how many groups receive airtime on MTV and the talent of these groups. For example, you may discuss the new dance groups. These groups generally do not play instruments, but offer the audience a great choreographed show--e.g., Cover Girls, Sweet Sensation, and Seduction.

THE LOOK OF THE SOUND

Pat Aufderheide

<u>Questions for Study and Discussion (p. 586)</u>

1. Music videos are defined in the first paragraph as "pioneers in video expression."

2. Videos are pioneers because they create new boundaries by eliminating the old. They are commercial and program in one. The programs are a "nonstop sequence of discontinuous episodes." They have also set themselves apart from television by being displayed in department stores and movie theatres.

3. MTV is successful because it "offers not only videos, but environment, a context that creates mood." The moods that videos reflect are "nostalgia, regret, anxiety, confusion, dread, envy, admiration, pity, titillation." They achieve this mood through the quick pace, the look of the VJs, the interesting sets and lighting, and the channel's populist attitude.

4. First Aufderheide presents her thesis that videos are "pioneers." Then she shows the ways in which videos have no boundaries. She follows with the suggestion that videos are packages of desire, then explains the reason for their success and how they are crafted to that end. She then proposes that videos are dreams, providing the fantasy she had earlier suggested in her idea that videos are packages of desire. She ends by bringing her argument full

circle with the suggestion that videos have no boundaries.

5. Videos are purely alternatives, they have no beginnings, no endings, and no past. Dreams create "gestalts" or patterns of sensations.

6. Aufderheide supports her argument through examples of videos and MTV antics, and quotes from MTV executives, video producers, video critics, professors of communication, and the National Coalition on Television Violence. Her use of quotes is most effective. Aufderheide did not merely watch television and extract examples that support her ideas. Instead, she has researched relevant books, magazines, producers, and management. The fact that these people can support her argument makes it more convincing than if she had merely spewed self-obtained examples.

7. As videos have crossed the boundaries of single episode, program, and commercial, they have also crossed the boundary between male and female.

8. Cross promotion occurs in commercials when celebrities promote themselves, the product, and any other product they may endorse. She uses Michael Jackson and Christie Brinkley as examples. Cross promotion brings two worlds together resulting in "not only a way of seeing and hearing but of being."

Writing Topics (p. 586)

1. It may be interesting to share the results of this assignment with the class, comparing the male responses with the female responses.

2. It may be helpful to discuss student's interpretations of this quote in class. This will help students organize their thoughts and serve as a focus for their ideas.

3. It may be helpful to discuss the fashion of videos in class as some students may not have MTV available to them in college dorms. Are there different fashions for different types of music, or is the fashion basically the same? Do the malls exploit the fashions used on MTV? These questions will serve a basis for discussion of this topic so students can focus their ideas for their essay.

SIN, SUFFER, AND REPENT

Donna Woolfolk Cross

Questions for Study and Discussion (p. 594)

1. This anecdote sets the tone of sarcasm and absurdity for the rest of the essay.

2. Not only do viewers confuse actors with their characters, they also use soap operas as a guide for their own lives, which can be detrimental to someone trying to work out a problem.

3. Cross offers facts outside the essay to clarify her point and for any reader who chooses to read them. If these facts were inserted into the essay, it could change the tone and the pace and bog down the argument.
    4. The ideal woman wants to get married and have children, would never dream of having an abortion and hopefully will never suffer a miscarriage. However, once she gives birth, she ignores her baby and her career and gives all her energy to pleasing her man.
    5. Cross uses hyperbole to explain soap opera children's growth stages. However, since the growth stages on soaps really are exaggerated, her use of hyperbole is humorous rather than ridiculous.
    6. There are no blue-collar workers. Only the upper class exists, so there are no social problems. Houses are immaculate, and no one suffers from simple problems such as flat feet or tooth aches.
    7. Cross is not only unopposed to soaps (as long as the viewer can separate soap life from reality); she seems to enjoy them. The following statements support this idea: "One can hardly blame her" (1), and "It was enough to unhinge anybody."

Writing Topics (p. 594)

1. As a prewriting activity you may want to ask these questions in class to soap-watchers and those who do not watch soaps. Then you may want the avid soap-watchers to decide how their soap opera has changed since the article was written; are the soaps taking a more responsible social position, or are they simply fulfilling fantasies?
    2. It may be helpful to hold a class discussion about the numerous investigative talk shows that claim to reveal the "real story" such as "Geraldo," "Inside Edition," and "A Current Affair." You may ask the students to decide to what extent these shows are representing "real life."

7 / NATURE AND SCIENCE

The Abundance of Nature

IN THE JUNGLE

Annie Dillard

Questions for Study and Discussion (p. 603)

1. In folklore, art and other human expressions, trees are a symbol of the center or source of life. As Dillard writes predominantly about nature, trees serve as a reasonable as well as an aesthetic central idea.

2. This statement shows the Manhattan writer's dilemma: he does not want to leave the Napo River, but is unsure why he wants to stay. By sharing the writer's thoughts with her readers, Dillard reveals her own inner struggle.

3. The jungle is beautiful, but it is also deadly, and Dillard does not spare us the frightening details. The bugs, the bats and the larger-than-life mammals make it sound like a less than ideal vacation spot.

4. Beginning in paragraph 15, Dillard's tone is harsh and disapproving when she describes the technology that has intruded into the Napo River environment. This harshness contrasts with the calmer more serene tone she uses to describe the jungle in its untouched splendor.

5. Dillard's metaphor likens the Napo River Basin to the most elemental of necessities, the need for food and drink. The metaphor brings the reader full circle to the beginning of the essay and shows how the Valley is more than it seems to be at first sighting: "It is not out of the way. It is in the way. . . ."

Writing Topics (p. 603)

1. Students need not describe a wooded area or a brook; they can illustrate places such as an amusement park, or a more concrete place as Boston Harbor, Central Park, or Rodeo Drive. These examples may serve as ideas for students who are having trouble with the focus of their essay.

2. As a prewriting activity, students may be encouraged to research the work of Marilyn French, in which she addresses the effects of human materialism on nature.

SNOWY

Robert Finch

Questions for Study and Discussion (p. 608)

1. Finch was less taken by the owl's beauty when he first encountered her than he was by the challenge of getting close enough to observe her.

2. A "flight year" designates the year in which a bird returns to a specific location after an absence of more than one year. After one year at any location the owl's prey is depleted enough that they cannot return for five years. In 1926-27, 2300 snowy owls were shot by Americans. Subsequently, the snowy owl was declared a protected species.

3. It is when the out-of-the-ordinary occurs that we experience elation. For example, it is more exciting to sight a snowy now that it is a protected species and its appearance is less common than it was when the bird was common.

4. A description of the bird's surroundings gives us clues about the bird just as the setting of a story will provide background and meaning for the actions of the characters.

5. Finch uses metaphor and simile to describe the owl's actions and personification to describe the beach. The metaphors clarify his ideas and the personification works sharply to make him the intruder in this isolated setting.

6. In paragraph 14, Finch explains how the Cape reminds the bird of her home.

7. Finch explains that the owl succeeds in outfoxing him by her camouflage, gliding through the air swiftly and effortlessly, and resembling "hidden strength and violence." He explains that her actions are "deliberate," are of "sheer, cool competence." He also explains that her beautiful ruse reveals her nature as a creature who is neither "slothlike or unaware." Finch shows his admiration for the bird in a portrait that is respectful and beautiful.

8. In this passage Finch compares his and the owl's mental capabilities. He seems to feel that the bird has it over him in strength of character and cunning.

Writing Topics (p. 608)

1. You may have students review the works of Annie Dillard (particularly Pilgrim at Tinker Creek) to see how other writers approach nature.

2. As a prewriting activity you may refer the students to selections under the heading "The Attack on Nature" in which the authors deal specifically with our "destruction" of nature and its effects on animals. Students may get a greater appreciation for the loss of species and the impact this has on the earth by reading some of these selections. This may help students formulate opinions and organize their thoughts for this assignment.

THE ANALOGOUS BEE

William Longgood

Questions for Study and Discussion (p. 613)

1. Humans resemble bees in their sloppy workmanship, useless endeavor, poor management, faulty judgment, reward systems, attitudes on age, elaborate social structure, and specialization of labor. Humans are unlike bees in that bees have a good sense of mission, react violently to ingratitude and treachery, have little sentiment, are socialists, hold no private goods, are consistently dedicated, self-sacrificing, not sexually driven, and well-organized, and provide no retirement, pension, or welfare. Bees are also different for having a built-in defense system and they

will unite as a hive to come to the aid of one of their members who is threatened by an outside danger.

2. A "cleansing flight" refers to bees' excursions outside the hive for the purpose of relieving themselves.

3. This motto--"work or die"--does not apply to human society. As Longgood says, "from the moment of a bee's 'birth' she is destined to work until she no longer can do so." She then commits suicide, departs, or is killed "by those she served so faithfully while she could." Bees live for one purpose, to maintain the species. This contrasts with the human purpose which has grown far more complex and, in some cases, seems bent on the destruction of the community instead of its enhancement.

4. It may seem surprising for Longgood to compare humans to bees if for no other reason than the difference in size and appearance makes them unlikely analogous creatures. Nevertheless, his comparison and contrast is delightfully convincing, makes it easier to visualize the activity of the hive and best of all gives the reader something new to think about.

5. The last sentences of a paragraph flow like warm honey directly into the next paragraph and move the argument along easily and clearly.

Writing Topics (p. 613)

1. As a means for generating ideas and information for this assignment, you can conduct a discussion in which you analyze both the positive and negative aspects of competition. Try to ascertain, as a group, just when a positive feature, if carried too far, can ultimately prove destructive, or just what the result might be if all competition were removed from our lives. You may then ask students to answer the question, "Is workaholism a product of competition, or something else?" Your discussion should yield some interesting points and provocative examples for students to keep in mind as they write their essays.

2. As a prewriting activity you may ask students to privately define "the perfect socialist society." Once they have done so, you may combine all the ideas on the board for a more comprehensive definition. Students may then use this definition as a point of reference for their papers. Students may then apply Longgood's examples of bee hives to their definition of a socialist society.

FIRST OBSERVATIONS

Jane Van Lawick-Goodall

Questions for Study and Discussion (p. 620)

1. The more we know about the observer, the more we will understand not only her results, but the methodology

she employs to get those results.

2. It is not necessary for Van Lawick-Goodall to explain each location as her description of each helps the reader visualize the habitat. Knowing that Van Lawick-Goodall is in Africa, the foreign-sounding names allow the reader to exercise a bit of imagination and to grasp the total "otherness" of this world.

3. The anecdotes not only allow Van Lawick-Goodall to contrast chimp and cat behavior; they allow her to compare chimp and human behavior.

4. Van Lawick-Goodall's argument that naming the chimps allows her to remember them more easily seems the stronger argument, except that later in her essay it is clear that she is guilty of anthropomorphicizing her chimps.

5. It may surprise some students to learn that chimpanzees build their nests every night and that they are fastidious enough to defecate and urinate over the edge of their nests. It seems entirely human, as does their tool making. Students may also be surprised to learn that chimps are carnivores since we are inclined to think of them as banana eaters. Their friendly disposition is not as surprising because we have read and seen enough about them to know that they are not considered dangerous creatures.

6. Van Lawick-Goodall discovers the chimpanzees eating a piglet and modifying a twig to dig out termites. The observations are exciting because it challenges long-held beliefs about chimpanzees.

7. Chimpanzees cannot be called "toolmakers" because that is the distinction that scientists make between man and all the other creatures. It follows that if chimps are toolmakers too, there is little difference between man and the lower beasts.

Writing Topics (p. 621)

1. As the question states, you may want to review the various aspects of narration with the class. It may also be important to review how Van Lawick-Goodall uses narration in her writing. After this discussion students may use Van Lawick-Goodall's style as a guide in writing their essay.

2. One way students may approach this assignment is to compare and contrast man and chimpanzees. They may get information from anthropology and zoology professors and draw conclusions of their own from their comparisons.

3. Students may find the definition of toolmaker to be unnecessarily broad, and as a result the definition of man is unnecessarily narrow. Consider philosophy which distinguishes man from the lower animals, variously as a moral creature, a discriminating creature, or as one capable of a spiritual relationship with his cosmos. Students may approach anthropologists on campus to learn if "toolmaker" is the only way they distinguish man from the other animals.

THE GRIZZLY

John McPhee

Questions for Study and Discussion (p. 624)

1. McPhee explains that a grizzly can weigh up to 600 pounds, with a fifty-five-inch waist and a thirty-inch-neck. The anecdote in paragraph 7 also graphically conveys the awesomeness of the grizzly's power.

2. In paragraph 6, McPhee explains that grizzlies are intelligent and their actions are independent of their moods.

3. McPhee wants to convey a sense of nature's awesomeness and integrity. He will find his audience among those who are interested in maintaining a relationship with the wild that is characterized by those very qualities.

4. McPhee and his companions are nature-lovers and advocates. McPhee explains in paragraph 7 the reasons it is dangerous to venture into grizzly territory with a gun. His argument seems tenuous unless he means to convey that a man carrying a gun will rely on it at the expense of keeping a sharp awareness of the grizzly's movements.

5. Eskimos know that grizzlies stalk. McPhee feels much the way the eskimos do. He fears and reveres them. Students will find endless examples of McPhee's diction to support this position.

Writing Topics (p. 624)

1. As the role of motivation is important in behavior, this assignment is asking students what motivates them into certain behavior. You may ask students to choose their focus carefully so that they may be realistic in their interpretation of their own motivation and so they may learn something about themselves. By sharing the responses with the class, they may also understand what motivates others as well.

2. You may ask students to consider the following: Do animals watch humans? Does our mental capacity to analyze make it difficult to speculate on what animals "think" since we don't know what their minds are capable of? Once the students come to a determination of how animal minds function differently than humans, they may be able to answer the questions posed in order to organize their thoughts for this assignment.

O sweet spontaneous earth

e. e. cummings

Questions for Study and Discussion (p. 627)

1. All the disciplines cummings names want to know
earth's "meaning." The earth replies simply . . . "spring."
This response is not only intended to make the reader aware
that earth is subtle and unself-conscious in her fulfillment
of herself, it also shows that the answer the scientists
seek is neither complex nor hidden except as a result of
their blindness.
2. The alliteration for "p," "th," "c," create rhythm
more than they lend meaning.
3. The sciences behave like an overbearing aunt or
grandmother who pinches and pokes at a child in a way meant
to be playful but which the child experiences as annoying
and embarrassing.
4. The "incomparable couch of death" refers to earth's
lover.
5. The mood of the poem is playful with cummings using
adjectives such as prurient, scraggy, and naughty to poke
fun at philosophy, science, and religion.

Writing Topics (p. 627)

1. As a prewriting activity you may divide the class
into three groups, each to discuss the ways in which either
science, religion, or philosophy answers the questions "why
and how?" Once each group reports to the class how their
discipline approaches answering "why and how" the class may
determine what e. e. cummings's response to each group might
have been. Then the students may, in their essays, determine which "answer" is best suited for the task.
2. Students unfamiliar with poems celebrating "spring"
or nature in general may refer to the works of the English
Romantics such as John Keats and William Wordsworth, or the
American Romantics such as William Cullen Bryant.

The Attack on Nature

THE BIG GOODBYE

David Quammen

Questions for Study and Discussion (p. 633)

1. Quammen's fantasy beginning points out that the
course of human events is leading inevitably to the extinction of the species. Since the self-destruction of the
species is the point of Quammen's essay, the beginning is

130

entirely appropriate. Students should take note that this beginning grabs Homo sapiens by the collar, along with all other extinct species, allowing it no escape on the grounds of being "different" from other animal forms.

2. The end of an era occurs over time; it does not occur in one day. However, the loss of Martha is significant because she died from the loss of her habitat, not from being hunted out of existence. So, although humans have been causing extinctions since before the seventeenth century, the pigeon signifies the start of a great line of extinctions caused by humans' technological advancement.

3. In paragraph 7, Quammen states that the pattern and rate of extinction are relevant to biological stability, defined "as extinctions occurring no more rapidly than new species arise." The Late Quaternary Period is unique for killing off almost a species a year, while it takes 10,000 years for a new one to arise.

4. Quammen's sarcasm and wit is an interesting counterpoint to the dramatic and frightening message he delivers. The effect is a mocking of the people he is addressing, as if to say, "What else should we expect from Homo sapiens?" He allows his reader no escape into complacency, nor should his tone be mistaken for a lack of seriousness. In truth, he is really very angry.

5. Quammen also uses dashes, ellipses, fantasy, glib phrasing and a plethora of examples to hold the reader's attention.

6. Poisoning estuaries, drilling oil, mowing rain forests, lumbering, and slash-and-burn agriculture have led to the destruction of many animal and plant habitats. The stated motivations for some of these activities are to support the fast food industry, the manufacture of trinkets, and the survival of the oil industry. The less obvious motivation is greed.

7. If Quammen really holds out no hope for the species, then his purpose in writing the essay is unclear. Perhaps, his real intent is to spur the reader to an "Oh yeah? Yes, we can save this planet" defiance of his attack.

8. The dictionary compares the "Dodo" to a large turkey while the slang term is "slow witted person." It is a perfect ending because Quammen is essentially calling mankind a dull-witted turkey.

Writing Topics (p. 633)

1. When students have both arguments, you may have them determine at what point it will be necessary to "change our ways." Some professors may not agree that we are without hope on our crash course toward doomsday, but may feel that we need to change our ways if we are going to live decently on earth.

2. To expand on this assignment, you may have students speculate what specifically about today's society has led to this author's "solutions" for the future. For example, the

131

ozone problem may be remedied by building societies in bubbles that will not be affected by the atmosphere. The student may have fun interpreting the causes of other science fiction settings.

THE ASSAULT ON WHALES

Jacques-Yves Cousteau and Yves Paccalet

Questions for Study and Discussion (p. 638)

1. At the beginning of their essay, the authors claim "the whale is the most astonishing animal the earth has ever known" (1). Although this claim may seem fantastic, they support it by describing the whale's most awesome and generally unknown qualities. "It would take 25 elephants, or 2,000 human beings, to equal the weight of a single blue whale" (1); "this mountain of muscle and fat is fluid as the element it calls home" (2); it is "gregarious, intelligent, peaceable . . . comes to the defense of its fellow whales." The authors also point out that whales are capable of conversing and singing.

2. Whaling advocates argue that jobs and essential protein would be lost if whales could not be hunted. The authors are convincing in countering these arguments with statistics of their own. They report that whaling and related industries employ less than a few thousand people across the world. (See paragraph 8 for a complete list of the statistics.) And in Japan, consumption of whale protein amounts to a mere 0.9 percent of the total protein intake.

3. Newly developed organizations, such as the International Whaling Commission, have formed to safeguard the whale. In addition, societal priorities are changing. For example, "manufactured consumer goods--are becoming commonplace, while commodities once plentiful and free--clean air and water, nature in all its exuberance--are growing scarce." Students may point out that of these two, The Whaling Commission will have the longest lasting effect on the future of whales, because societal attitudes are ever-changing. The irony expressed in paragraph 13 is that the wholesale slaughter of whales has made the species difficult to find and kill.

4. "We owe it to ourselves, to our children, and to generations yet unborn," to save whales because, "if we lose the whales, we lose something of incalculable value from our dreams, our myths, our finest poetry--from all the things that made us human before we defined ourselves in terms of heavy industry."

5. The authors' diction shows respect and awe for the whale and distrust of its hunters. They describe the whale as "most astonishing animal," "living superlative," "mountain of muscle," "fluid," "wondrous [form] of life." They describe the acts of killing the whales as a "massacre,"

132

that deprives "our dreams" . . . it is a "butchery." Their apparent anger is not a deterrent to their essay since it is supported by hard facts.

6. The first two paragraphs describe the whale and present it as a "wondrous life form." Paragraphs 4-6 explain their disdain for mankind's killing of whales. The next four paragraphs explain other's rationalizations for the continued "killing for profit" of whales. The next four paragraphs explain what changes are occurring that may work to safeguard the whale. The next paragraphs, however, make it clear that caution is still necessary because of environmental risks. The final paragraphs offer a poetic argument for the preservation of the whales. The organization is clean and allows the reader to follow the argument with ease. The authors have explained whales' impact on human life, but the argument may benefit from a discussion of their impact on marine life and the losses to marine life that would follow the whales' extinction.

7. The Whaling Commission may have to address the void created in the marine life ecosystem and food chain if whales are killed off. It may address the phenomenon of excessive blood filling the ocean when whales are killed. And since pollution is a factor in whales' deaths, it may also have to address the problem of pollution.

Writing Topics (p. 638)

1. As a prewriting activity you may use these questions as a focus of discussion so that students may hear views other than their own. You may also review with the class the authors' style of argument so that they may use the essay as a reference for organizing their own essays.

2. As a prewriting activity you may ask students to speak out about topics they feel strongly about, whether it be recycling, acid rain, car pooling, animal rights, the greenhouse effect, or others. You may ask students who do not voice a concern why they are not concerned.

FEAR IN A HANDFUL OF NUMBERS

Dennis Overbye

Questions for Study and Discussion (p. 643)

1. This expression is generally intended to mean that we cannot change the everyday weather. However, Overbye suggests that we do in fact affect the weather by virtue of our carelessness.

2. Overbye's audience, the readers of Time magazine, is the lay public, albeit an educated, sophisticated one. The cowboy and Indian analogy is particularly fitting because the duo conjures an image of eternal struggle in the uniquely "true grit" American style.

3. In paragraph 3, Overbye asks four questions which he answers almost immediately by insisting that we take action to save our earth. His notion, of "pretending" until a "real" commitment hits, seems reasonable if you believe, as cognitive therapists do, that thought precedes action. Thus we can work to change our thoughts and as a result, change our action.

4. Pollution kills our habitat without which we will eventually die.

5. Overbye uses the following metaphors: "Los Angelenos whipping their sunny basin into a brown blur on the way to work every morning" (1); "nature was metaphorically transformed. It became dead meat" (4); "victory over nature is a kind of suicide" (6); "what we have now is a sort of biological equivalent to a black hole" (6). Each of these metaphors helps clarify the author's ideas by putting them in terms the reader will understand. The metaphors have also been chosen to jolt the reader with a brutality that insists we don't have decades in which to ponder the fine points of the argument.

6. Although science is a "cowboy" achievement, it actually favors the "Indian" view of nature as alive.

7. For Overbye numbers can help us "read" the progress of our self destruction. Overbye suggests that we need more science to calculate the hazards we are creating and make us aware of the problems we face. Overbye is therefore offering science, not as progress, but as a picture of reality. Thus he resolves the seeming contradiction in suggesting that science step forward to solve the problems of a too rapid progress.

8. "Payment" for our prosperity and taking what we want will be the courage to make do with less as a means of persuading the rest of the world to do likewise.

9. Rather than argue for the typical conservations that environmentalists plead, Overbye suggests that we change our frame of mind, that we "pretend."

Writing Topics (p. 644)

1. Students may discuss Overbye's arguments with a professor of environmental studies to get a second opinion on what options, if any, are feasible in counteracting the greenhouse effect. By researching feasible options students can answer for themselves who should be approached to eliminate the effects and what success can be expected.

2. As a prewriting activity you may find it helpful to compare the two writers' styles in class. You may then ask students how they would contrast the causes and effects of these two types of pollution. Answering these questions may serve as a focus for the students to begin their essay.

DANCING WITH NATURE

Don Mitchell

<u>Questions for Study and Discussion (p. 652)</u>

1. By the end of his essay, Mitchell has not only defined the "nature writer," he has defined "nature" and his relationship to it in a new and unexpected way.

2. In paragraphs 1-15, Mitchell uses a point-by-point comparison of the "nature writer" to the "non-nature writer" to arrive at a definition of them both. In paragraphs 16-21, he uses a system of classification to distinguish among nature writers. In paragraphs 27-34, he classifies three grounds for error in nature writing, and he concludes his essay with a plea for an honest engagement with nature. His organization is appropriate, since he reveals as thorough and authentic an engagement with his subject as he advocates for "nature writers." In other words, in his very presentation of his subject Mitchell practices what he preaches.

3. In paragraph 4, Mitchell says that "nature writers are chiefly concerned with something larger than human nature." Most students familiar with nature writing will probably agree that Mitchell has hit the mark with his definition, since it describes precisely that writing which offers the human observer only the smallest role in the drama.

4. Mitchell debunks the myth of nature as some "cosmic Mother," benevolent and nurturing. Students' opinions as to the validity of this observation will differ no doubt depending on their "engagement" with nature.

5. In general, Mitchell uses italicized words to emphasize and distinguish the finer points of his argument. For example, nature writers are concerned with something larger than <u>human</u> nature, which is to say the world <u>outside</u> the writer.

6. Dillard disappoints Mitchell for her failure to have fully engaged her subject, relying instead on the observations of other writers for some of her facts. The example he offers of her "error" strengthens his argument precisely because Annie Dillard is a well-known and respected "nature writer." That even she could make such a mistake underlines the risks to the reader that Mitchell warns us of.

7. Mitchell's title alludes to his concluding remarks in which he says that nature is a "necessary dancing partner." Such remarks come at the end of the essay because the author has allowed us to arrive at his conclusion when he did . . . at the end of an exploration of his thoughts on "nature."

1. Students may approach this assignment by drawing on
their own experience to compare and contrast the activities
associated with a passionate pursuit of a hobby to those
associated with a casual pursuit. Students should be reminded of the role specific examples will play in their
definitions.
2. Mitchell criticizes Dillard, using her as an example of what a nature writer is not. As a prewriting activity you may want to provide the students with a copy of
Pilgrim at Tinker Creek--particularly that section Mitchell
refers to--so they may determine for themselves whether
Dillard is a "nature writer." Finally, have students write
essays in which they attack or defend Mitchell's assessment
of Dillard. Encourage them to use examples from Dillard's
writing to illustrate their positions.

THE BIRTH-MARK

Nathaniel Hawthorne

Questions for Study and Discussion (p. 667)

1. The birthmark by its nature and by name is a visible reminder of Georgiana's birth. The hand is a further
reminder that she was born mortal with the hand of God upon
her. It is easy to extend the metaphor to all humans born
with the "stain" of mortality that some Christians refer to
as original sin.
2. Aylmer is the personification of romanticism with
his lonely search into the mystical reaches of the cosmos
and his fiddling with the natural order. His use of words
such as magic, alchemist, and my art, heighten his image as
a "sorcerer," as do the illusions he creates for his wife's
entertainment. Students will find many such references to
things emotional, dark, and magical in their reading of this
story.
3. The husband is, as Hawthorne says, "a type of the
spiritual element," who represents man's search for the
wisdom of the cosmos. Aminadab represents man's "physical
nature," the sensing creature who, content and somehow wiser
than the husband, said "If she were my wife, I'd never part
with that birthmark." The unfortunate wife is, as Hawthorne
describes Georgiana in the end, the embodiment of the "an-
gelic spirit (that) kept itself in union with a mortal
frame." Hawthorne seems to speak through her since clearly
her last words are meant to be the moral of the story.
4. Aylmer's fatal flaw is his pride, the "hubris" of
the Greeks, which blinds him to his limitations in God's
universe. First we are aware of his flaw by the way is
which it disturbs the noble character of his wife. Later,
Hawthorne foreshadows the tragedy. First, Aylmer fails at

several attempts to amuse Georgiana with magic flowers and a portrait. Throughout the story he brags of the terrible and dangerous concoctions he has brewed, adding that the one he is concocting for her "must go deeper." Finally, Georgiana reads accounts of his many experiments which ended in frightful failure. Aylmer's flaw is most graphically described, much as the man would have described his wife's blemish, as "intense thought had set its stamp upon every previous page of that volume; but the thoughts of years were all concentrated upon the last." The reader cannot help but see the husband tragically marked by his pride in a way that renders him fearsome and ugly, while his wife's mark leaves her only human.

5. Hawthorne's story is draped in emotion and rich, dark colors just as Georgiana's compartment was. And it is bathed in the pungent aroma of incense and the alchemist's furnace.

6. The ending of the tale was no surprise. The author makes his moral clear throughout the tale, and underlines it with the wife's last words. Georgiana's final statement reveals Hawthorne's message that the pursuit of scientific knowledge must not occur at the expense of nature. In his view, a scientist who allows his hubris to interfere with God's plan will only bring on his own destruction.

Writing Topics (p. 668)

1. As a prewriting activity you may hold a discussion about the "wonders" of science. Through such advances as genetic engineering, we seek perfection--in tomatoes, cows, pigs, and even humans. Students should determine whether they think this kind of experimentation is justifiable and whether it can be called "intellectual growth," or if these pursuits are merely an arrogant attempt to achieve perfection. They should consider which, if either, is ethical or moral.

2. As a prewriting activity you may discuss students' answers to question three above to determine the assistant's qualities, his role in the story, and his possible subsequent role in life. By sharing answers, students may find different qualities that they can relate to in themselves.

Some Classic Statements

THE DECLARATION OF INDEPENDENCE

Thomas Jefferson

Questions for Study and Discussion (p. 674)

1. The purpose of government, according to the Declaration, is "to secure" "certain unalienable Rights," among them "Life, Liberty, and the pursuit of Happiness" (2). These are of course individual rights, and governments also exist to serve other purposes--the adjudication of disputes, for example, and the protection of private property--that do not quite fit the Declaration's formulation. Presumably Jefferson did not feel the need to tell his readers what they already know and what does not, after all, have much to do with the reasons for revolt against England.

2. At the end of paragraph 2 Jefferson states that "The history of the present King of Great Britain is a history of repeated injuries and usurpations, all having in direct object the establishment of an absolute Tyranny over these States." Jefferson then lists the specific charges against the King in paragraphs 3-29.

3. The Declaration offers the argument in paragraph 2 that when a government is despotic it should be abolished and a new one established. The argument is based on the following premises: (a) "all men are created equal," (b) "they are endowed by their Creator with certain unalienable Rights," (c) "Governments are instituted" to secure these unalienable rights, and (d) people have a right and a duty to throw off a despotic government. Once these assumptions are accepted, the rest of Jefferson's argument follows logically.

4. In paragraph 31 Jefferson reviews the ways in which the colonies have attempted to make the British government aware of their problems.

5. Examples of Jefferson's emotionally charged language include wholesome (3), refused (5), inestimable (5), formidable (5), tyrants (5), manly (7), swarms (12), and harass (12). Having established a sound logical argument, Jefferson uses emotionally charged language to call forth feelings of patriotism among the colonists.

Writing Topics (p. 674)

1. Students will find that among other things, a powerful and lengthy condemnation of the slave trade was deleted from Jefferson's first draft. That clause began: "He has waged cruel war against human nature itself, violating its most sacred rights of life and liberty in the per-

sons of a distant people who never offended him, captivating and carrying them into slavery in another hemisphere, or to incur miserable death in their transportation hither." Since several states benefitted economically from slavery and would not support any document attacking that institution, the offending clause was removed--and all thirteen colonies adopted the Declaration.

2. One principle that was abandoned over a century ago is the right of the people to throw off a government they consider despotic; hence the Civil War, in which the federal government sought to regain its dominion over 11 states that seceded from the Union. Some students may also observe that we no longer think of Native Americans as "merciless Indian Savages, whose known rule of warfare, is an undistinguished destruction of all ages, sexes and conditions," and that American armed forces in various parts of the world have at times been no more merciful. Finally, the constant reference to the States in the plural reminds us that at the time there was no strong central government and that the states were then sovereign.

CIVIL DISOBEDIENCE

Henry David Thoreau

Questions for Study and Discussion (p. 692)

1. Thoreau's discussion of the possibilities and limitations of government appears in the first two paragraphs. He sees government, at best, as an expedient, "the mode which the people have chosen to execute their will. . . . Governments show . . . how successfully men can be imposed on, even impose on themselves, for their own advantage," but, he continues, "government is an expedient by which men would fain succeed in letting one another alone; and . . . when it is most expedient, the governed are most likely let alone by it."

Later in the essay Thoreau also states that governments can impose laws enforced by majority rule, but they cannot impose conscience within individuals and, ultimately, "It is not desirable to cultivate a respect for the law, so much as for the right" (4).

2. Thoreau was jailed for refusing to pay a poll-tax collected by the State. In paragraph 26 he describes why he considered himself free, even while in jail: "I could not but smile to see how industriously they locked the door on my meditations, which followed them out again without let or hindrance, and they were really all that was dangerous."

3. People should not obey laws they consider unjust, according to Thoreau, because "The only obligation which I have a right to assume is to do at any time what I think right" (4). The alternative is to surrender the dictates of conscience to the authority of the State or of majority

rule, neither of which is ultimately based on justice. Thoreau believes justice to be the product of the individual conscience, and only when individual consciences work together for the right, regardless of expediency or law, can a governing body be considered just. He writes: "Why has every man a conscience, then? I think we should be men first, and subjects afterwards. . . . It is truly enough said that a corporation has no conscience; but a corporation of conscientious men is a corporation with a conscience" (4).

4. Thoreau is sincere but demanding in his attitude against supporting the State when it participates in activities he finds unjust. His remarks are aimed mainly at the people of his community and of his state, and are an attempt to awaken them from an unthinking, too-facile allegiance to the State. In that attempt he does not mince words, as the following excerpts illustrate: "Those who, while they disapprove of the character and measures of a government, yield to it their allegiance and support are undoubtedly its most conscientious supporters, and so frequently the most serious obstacles to reform" (14); "How can a man be satisfied to entertain an opinion merely, and enjoy it?" (15); "I do not hesitate to say, that those who call themselves Abolitionists should at once effectively withdraw their support, both in person and property, from the government of Massachusetts, and not wait till they constitute a majority of one, before they suffer the right to prevail through them" (20).

5. Thoreau's purpose is to get others to act as he has, so that the State will be forced to discontinue its activities in support of slavery and the Mexican War. He is not merely trying to rationalize his own behavior since, as is clear throughout his essay, he has little regard for how people respond to his unorthodox behavior because he acts according to his conscience rather than to the expediency of law or public opinion.

6. Daniel Webster serves as an example of those statesmen and legislators who "standing so completely within the institution, never distinctly and nakedly behold it." According to Thoreau, "Webster never goes behind government, and so cannot speak with authority about it. . . . His quality is not wisdom, but prudence. . . . Notwithstanding his special acuteness and ability, he is unable to take a fact out of its merely political relations, and behold it as it lies absolutely to be disposed of by the intellect" (42).

Students' opinions on Thoreau's assessment of Webster may vary, and will likely suggest how they feel about Webster's single-minded devotion to the Constitution.

7. Thoreau uses a variety of techniques to support and document his claims. To give philosophical credence to the positions he maintains he refers to sources like the Bible, Shakespeare, and other philosophers and poets. He mentions the events that have taken place around him--in his community, in the state, and in the nation--to document his claims

about the injustice being done in regard to slavery and the Mexican War. And, finally, he uses his own experiences to support his views about the need for and justness of civil disobedience.

Writing Topics (p. 692)

1. As a prewriting activity designed to provide students with a body of information from which they can shape their essays for this topic, you can ask them to do research into examples of unjust imprisonments in recent history and then have them share the results of their work in class, discussing the context of Thoreau's statement as it applies to their examples. This type of classroom activity may help students formulate opinions about the validity of Thoreau's statement.

2. As a prewriting discussion for this topic you can ask students to consider Thoreau's statement, "The only obligation which I have a right to assume is to do at any time what I think right." Students have probably encountered examples, in their own lives or through news media, of situations where someone who felt he was doing right was also acting in a way extremely harmful to others or to society. Given such situations, find out how students would reconcile Thoreau's statement with the notion of public good or even public safety. Your discussion may yield some insights into the difficulties of reconciling individual conscience with majority rule.

3. As suggested in Writing Topic #1 for "Letter from Birmingham Jail" (see p. 145 in this manual), students can also research the works and writings of Mahatma Gandhi and consider how they relate to both Thoreau and King, especially since Gandhi's life falls between these other two.

DECLARATION OF SENTIMENTS AND RESOLUTIONS

Elizabeth Cady Stanton

Questions for Study and Discussion (p. 697)

1. Stanton no doubt wished to remind her listeners or readers of the moral basis on which our American system of government was established, while at the same time indicate that in the treatment of women that moral basis was not being upheld.

2. The intent of parody is to burlesque or criticize through humor the content or style of another work. Stanton is not interested in either in her treatment of the Declaration of Independence. She is very serious about drawing attention to the principles upon which our government rests, in order that she may point out how women have been excluded from the full benefit of those principles. Her presentation of "self-evident truths" suggests that she believes firmly

in the precepts outlined by Thomas Jefferson, and those
precepts provide a moral and civil basis for her fight for
women's rights. In short, parody means to undermine the
intent of the work it is modeled on, whereas Stanton wishes
instead to reinforce the meaning and importance of the
Declaration of Independence.

3. In general, the women at the Seneca Falls conven-
tion want it recognized that the great precept of Nature
that "man shall pursue his own true and substantial happiness," applies to men and women equally. A more specific
listing of individual demands related to that recognized
precept is presented in paragraphs 23-35.

4. The "elective franchise" is the right to vote. It
is fundamental to Stanton's argument because none of the
other issues she mentions can be addressed properly until
women are given an elective voice in establishing the conditions under which they are to live. As Stanton states in
paragraph 7, "Having deprived [woman] of this first right of
a citizen, the elective franchise, thereby leaving her
without representation in the halls of legislation, [man]
has oppressed her on all sides."

5. Stanton's statement refers to the fact that once
married, a woman's rights become secondary to those of her
husband, leaving her no legal recourse should she wish to
assert her rights independent of her husband's will.

6. Since, in paragraph 3, Stanton states that "The
history of mankind is a history of repeated injuries and
usurpations on the part of man toward woman, having in
direct object the establishment of an absolute tyranny over
her," the repeated references to "He" in the list of abuses
that follows indicates men, in general, through the history
of mankind.

The rhetorical effect of listing the abuses as she has,
and beginning each with "He," is an acute sense of emphasis,
and an escalating awareness of the extent to which men have
tyrannized women. There is also the reminder of the similar
use of "He" in reference to King George in the Declaration
of Independence, reinforcing this degree of tyranny.

7. As the final resolution in paragraph 35 suggests,
Stanton's declaration is aimed at both men and women.

8. If Stanton had concluded her declaration at paragraph 20, it would only have provided a list of grievances
and, therefore, created only a sense of destructive action
without an accompanying sense of constructive counteraction.
The list of resolutions provides a concrete description of
exactly how women wish to change the abusive conditions
outlined in paragraphs 4-18.

9. Students' responses to this question may vary. We
see no such indicators of "feminine" writing.

Writing Topics (p. 698)

1. As a prewriting activity for this topic, it may
be interesting to compare Stanton's declaration with the

founding doctrine or constitution of a currently active
women's organization like NOW (National Organization of
Women). Such a comparison should help students respond to
the questions of what issues still need to be addressed and
what new complaints have been voiced in the last 20 years.
A look at the debate surrounding attempts at passing the
Equal Rights Amendment may also provide useful information
in this regard.

2. In looking at Jefferson's document students can
substitute "women" for all the references to the American
colonists and "men" for all the references to England or
King George, to see what effect it has on their reading of
the Declaration, and how the Declaration would then compare
to Stanton's document. They may be surprised at how conve-
niently the substitutions can be made, and might therefore
be able to draw conclusions about Stanton's use of the
Declaration of Independence as the model for her own
Declaration of Sentiments and Resolutions.

MY PEOPLE

Chief Seattle

Questions for Study and Discussion (p. 701)

1. Chief Seattle's reply is addressed to Governor
Stevens and through him to the federal government, and is
read aloud to Seattle's assembled tribesmen. In the reply
he indicates that he will probably accept the government's
offer, reminds the government of its promise of protection
and justice, warns the government of the consequences of any
breach of the government's promises, and sets one condition
on his acceptance.

2. In paragraph 8 Seattle sets the following condition: "I here and now make this condition that we will not
be denied the privilege without molestation of visiting at
any time the tombs of our ancestors, friends and children."
He prepares for this condition by stating in paragraph 4:
"To us the ashes of our ancestors are sacred and their
resting place is hallowed ground."

3. Seattle shows a wary and ironic respect for white
men, their president, and their god, as evidenced in paragraphs 1 and 3. He refers to the president as a "father"
because, in the Indians' patriarchal society, the father is
the leader, but there is some irony here, as in this passage: "Our good father at Washington--for I presume he is
now our father as well as yours, since King George has moved
his boundaries further north" (3), as if such fatherhood
were a matter of geography rather than trust and allegiance.
Seattle knows that the president is "great" from his power
but can only "presume" that he is good--that is, that having
promised the Indians money for their land and enough living
space for their needs, he will keep that promise. For as

Seattle says, "the Red Man no longer has rights that he need respect" (1).

4. Most students will agree that paragraph 8 is the most powerful part of Seattle's speech. Its cadence, its eeriness, and its prophecies certainly contribute to its powerfulness. The most surprising part of the speech comes in paragraph 7 wherein Seattle says that in death the white man and the Indian may be brothers after all. This is surprising because in paragraph 3 Seattle says that "we are two distinct races with separate origins and separate destinies."

5. Seattle concentrates on differences of religion, attitudes toward the land, and attitudes toward nature. He undoubtedly concentrated on these differences because they are the most significant to him, and because they relate to the condition he is making for his acceptance of the government's offer. He omits other obvious differences, such as those concerning economics and government, because they are irrelevant to his overall purpose.

6. Seattle draws his analogies and metaphors from the world of nature. The white man, for example, is compared to "the grass that covers vast prairies," while the Indian is like "scattering trees" or the "receding tide." Seattle uses these figures of speech in the context of his belief that change is the law of nature and that one day the white man may find himself in the same position as the Indian.

Writing Topics (p. 702)

1. In the late 1830s during Andrew Jackson's administration the tribes of the southeast were driven west at bayonet point into unsettled territory, along what came to be called the "trail of tears." After Chief Seattle's death, the settling of the American interior continued and the Plains tribes were subjugated, often bloodily. Students looking for library sources will find them under the subject heading Indians of North America--History and related topical and geographic subheadings.

2. Students tackling this question would do well to familiarize themselves in some detail with the previous and subsequent history of the Suquamish Indians and other tribes of the region. They will find information under the subject heading Indians of North America--Northwest, Old. A leader such as Chief Seattle would have to consider what is best for his people, not merely what he personally would prefer to do--but perhaps some students may find that resistance was a rational, even promising alternative.

144

LETTER FROM BIRMINGHAM JAIL

Martin Luther King, Jr.

Questions for Study and Discussion (p. 716)

1. King wrote the letter in response to a statement by fellow clergymen that his activities were "unwise and untimely." King was in Birmingham at the request of the Alabama Christian Movement for Human Rights; he led nonviolent demonstrations--sit-ins and marches--against racism and segregation and was arrested for these efforts as an "outside agitator."

2. King believed that he stood in the middle, between the forces of complacency and acceptance and those of bitterness and violence. His middle-ground consisted of active non-violent efforts to oppose and end segregation.

3. King sees the contemporary church as too often "an archdefender of the status quo" (30), whereas the early church acted as a "thermostat that transformed the mores of society" (37).

4. The objection that he was an "outsider" did not apply because King had been invited to Birmingham, because injustice was there, and because no citizen of America can be an "outsider" within its boundaries.

In response to the objection concerning direct-action and demonstrations, King replies that these activities are meant to oppose injustice and violence, not initiate them. He describes in detail the orderly process of such activities.

To the charge of "untimeliness" he quotes Niebuhr: "Justice too long delayed is justice denied."

He responds to the anxiety that he and his organization are breaking laws by quoting Augustine's "an unjust law is no law at all."

He demonstrates the illogic of the charge that peaceful action precipitates violence; he identifies Christ, Amos, and St. Paul as fellow extremists; and he protests the commendations of the Birmingham police's public behavior by providing examples of their private brutality.

5. King calls upon the clergy to respond in an active, aggressive way to alleviate racism and end segregation. He wishes them to honor the basic tenets of Christianity and the fundamentals of the Constitution and the Declaration of Independence.

6. King views racism and segregation as forms of spiritual violence. He recommends that people oppose this violence by peacefully resisting oppression, demonstrating against it with direct action in the form of sit-ins and marches. He responds to the praise of the Birmingham police by revealing their brutal private behavior and condemning their purpose, the preservation of "the evil system of segregation."

7. King's audience is the general public, both white

and African-American, who need to be informed of the intents
and purposes of the nonviolent movement. Though sorely
tried, King avoids anger, bitterness, or harangue. He pays
careful attention to the potential prejudices and objections
of his audience, and consistently maintains a reasonable,
even gentlemanly, tone.

Writing Topics (p. 717)

1. In preparation for this assignment students may
also wish to seek out information on the works and writings
of India's Mahatma Gandhi, and see what applications they
can find in his actions and ideas of principles taken from
Thoreau. They can then compare Gandhi's writings on nonviolent resistance to Martin Luther King's "Letter from Birmingham Jail," to see if the two men have interpreted
Thoreau's principle of civil disobedience in the same
manner.
2. As a prewriting activity for this topic you can
discuss nonviolent resistance and its alternatives in connection with a current battle being waged to bring about
social or legal change. The recent activities of anti-
abortion advocates can serve as a good focus for such a
discussion, since these advocates represent a wide range of
opinions about how to attack the abortion issue. Having
students do a bit of research on the matter before they come
to class may generate more specific information about the
tactics proposed by the various anti-abortion groups, and
may in turn provide students with a concrete base of information from which to consider the issue of nonviolent resistance in light of its alternatives.

THE UNKNOWN CITIZEN

W. H. Auden

Questions for Study and Discussion (p. 719)

1. The poem is ironic, as is revealed by the exaggerated materialism of lines 18-21, the doctrinaire complacency
of lines 22-24, and the joke in line 27, for example--no-
body, not even the most obtuse statistician, would say such
things in public. The views are those of the State (which
erected the monument on which the poem is said to be inscribed), which here has the voice and soul of the insensitive paper-pushers and statisticians of contemporary bureaucracy.
2. Whatever is inscribed on a public monument usually
reflects not only the State's view but also majority public
opinion, so Auden is able to satirize not only the bureaucratic outlook but also the materialistic values of a large
segment of contemporary society. The title suggests that
just as the military virtues of bravery and self-sacrifice

are celebrated through the Unknown Soldier, likewise the peacetime "virtues" of political docility and consumption of goods can be embodied in the Unknown Citizen.

3. We are given some objective information about the Citizen: where he worked, for example, and that he paid his dues, reacted normally to advertisements, carried a health-card, used the installment plan, owned basic appliances, was married, and raised five children. However, the poem omits all mention of the Citizen's feelings and aspirations, except to dismiss the subject in the last two lines; what the State has not "heard" and cannot quantify is unimportant. Since the poem is ironic, however, we can conclude almost by definition that Auden's attitudes and values are the opposite of the State's.

4. Since the Citizen's identification number is given he is not really unknown, but the inscription strips away his individuality and humanity. (Alert students may notice the hidden rhyme 8/State.)

5. Through his use of capitals, Auden is implying that the state has reified abstractions--and at the same time, by capitalizing such mundane expressions as "Installment Plan," he is mocking that tendency.

6. Auden must have intended his readers to join him in his dislike of bureaucracy, and also no doubt in his contempt for materialism. The bland effrontery of the last two lines would surely anger most readers, and the suggestion that a few household appliances are "everything necessary to the Modern Man" (20) is so reductive as to compel opposition.

Writing Topics (p. 719)

1. Many students will enjoy updating Auden's satire of the materialistic, conformist citizen and substituting contemporary references. This assignment also provides the opportunity for a discussion of generalizations and stereotypes.

2. This activity, a variant on the ever-popular assignment to "write your own obituary," asks students to consider what they would be most proud to have achieved. Also, since they are writing of themselves in third person, they are required to objectify themselves, choosing an appropriate tone and selecting details that would be of general public interest.

3. The information the government collects directly through census, tax, draft, and medical forms is often essential for planning and funding public programs. But many worry that such information may be misused by government or improperly leaked to private inquirers. In preparation for this assignment, therefore, you can discuss with students exactly what information the government has about them, what constructive purposes that information might serve, and what harm might be done by its improper use. You

can also examine how the growth in electronic information recording and storage has facilitated the government's capacity to collect such data, and to what ultimate effect.

THE YELLOW WALLPAPER

Charlotte Perkins Gilman

Questions for Study and Discussion (p. 734)

1. The heroine tires from writing, entertaining, traveling, "controlling" herself, following the pattern in the wallpaper, and finally even from trying to think clearly. In short, she is emotionally weary and is suffering a severe depression.

2. The paper is drab. It lacks a pattern or a plan, as does the heroine's life. The two patterns represent the inner and outer selves of women of that era. Specifically, the front pattern represents the attitudes and behavior proper to a "good wife," while the back pattern represents the imaginative, emotional self that women of Gilman's time were expected to keep "under control."

3. The woman describes her husband first as "practical," having "no patience with faith," but a nurturing and caring man. She respects him and does what she can to appease him without making any real judgment about how his treatment of her contributes to her illness. Later however, she grows suspicious of John and even a "little afraid." He seems "queer" to her but she attributes it to the wallpaper. Finally, he is the enemy, "as if I couldn't see through him" and she is free "in spite of" him and Jane.

4. The wife is suffering a nervous breakdown, either as the result of post-partum depression or from the effects of a sheltered and oppressive life. But because her condition is grounded in mental rather than physical causes, and because her husband has removed all that he believes would cause her to suffer, John cannot believe that her condition is serious.

5. The husband is very nurturing, but acts more as a father than a husband. He says, "what is it little girl?" when he catches her up late at night, and refers to her childlike habits of "imaginative power and habit of story making." Meanwhile the wife makes reference to her need for stimulation, a change of scene and secrecy. She is stronger and more in touch with her needs than her husband gives her credit for.

6. As the story progresses the wife becomes more and more involved with the paper, which of course is a metaphor for her condition. At first she merely dislikes it. Then it takes on human qualities and she sees things moving in the paper. Soon the paper is all she can think about. The people around her change from nurturing to sinister in her eyes and the room she abhorred becomes her refuge. Her

tragic decline is marked by the repeating of words such as "nervous," and phrases such as: "I cry at nothing" (90); "There are things in that paper that nobody knows but me, or ever will" (122); "torturing" (144); "I wonder if they all come out of that wallpaper as I did?" (245). Gilman moves the story along at a fast enough pace that we see the swift, yet smooth decline of the wife.

7. The word "creep" connotes sneaking. In the context of the story, the women "creep" to avoid detection and the forced return to the despised way of life.

8. Just as she sneaks her writing, the woman sneaks her fantasies about the wallpaper. Nothing about the wallpaper is revealed to the husband, and she does not tell him she writes. Both activities are symbolic and real manifestations of her crumbling independence.

9. The woman soon grows to like the room because of the wallpaper. The change in attitude signifies her "going over the edge." She is afraid to go outside because the woman is out there. As the woman creeps, so would she and it is embarrassing to have others see you "creep" in the daylight. The woman escapes from her husband into madness and so has the final, terrible victory.

Writing Topics (p. 734)

1. As a prewriting activity you may want to discuss post-partum depression and how a feminist would react to someone terming the heroine's condition as a hormone imbalance. It may also be useful to discuss Gilman's purpose in writing this story.

2. Answering the list of questions will serve to focus students on one topic for their assignment and organize their thoughts. Students may also wish to consider how Gilman's thoughts have informed feminism today, and how her ideas are visible in contemporary feminist writing.

Contemporary Issues

THE HUMAN COST OF AN ILLITERATE SOCIETY

Jonathan Kozol

Questions for Study and Discussion (p. 744)

1. Kozol sets a tone of urgency by letting the reader speculate on the dangers an illiterate faces everyday in every aspect of life.

2. Kozol recounts daily situations requiring an ability to read which are faced by all illiterates. He is convincing when he shows that all aspects of daily life demand an ability to read. For example, he tells of one illiterate who was stranded after his car broke down because he could

not tell the police where he was.

3.   Kozol implies that a lack of wealth and privilege, and prejudice, having the "wrong color" skin, contribute to illiteracy.

4.   According to Kozol, an illiterate society will be unable to uphold and defend Democracy and will, in a society dependent upon the written word, be at the mercy of others who are literate.

5.   Kozol makes a rational appeal using convincing examples of the many ways illiterates are at a disadvantage in daily social situations. However, some students may argue that the problem is not as extreme for all illiterates.

6.   Kozol does not give illiterates credit for remembering and verbalizing. Illiteracy is not linked to I.Q. in all cases. For example, renting an apartment should not be difficult for an intelligent person whether he can read or write or not. Most people know what the rent will be long before they sign the lease.

7.   Throughout the essay Kozol provides examples that portray illiterates as defenseless, economically deprived, disenfranchised, and unable to participate in the system.

Writing Topics (p. 744)

1.   As a prewriting activity you may encourage students to research the works of PLUS--Project Literacy U.S. The students may contact different chapters of PLUS that deal with different areas of the nation or their state to discern where the problem areas are and if the solution to literacy is the same in these problem areas as in the less afflicted areas.

2.   This is a good assignment to make the students aware of the problem in "their" world. It is very easy to recognize that a problem exists, but it is not so easy to realize that it exists so close to home. First-hand accounts from professors or students that illiteracy occurs on college campuses could enlighten some students.

WHAT WE KNOW ABOUT THE HOMELESS

Thomas Main

Questions for Study and Discussion (p. 758)

1.   Levey defended Joyce Brown in her fight against hospital policy to show that precisely these kinds of bureaucratic policies reinforce the plight of the poor in our culture. Some students may feel that people like Joyce Brown do not have the right to choose to live on the streets if they will endanger the health and well-being of others.

2.   Joyce Brown explains that Project Help had never "been of any use, except to offer her a sandwich," and she

fought any effort to move her "inside." However, in taking
the sandwich from Project Help, Joyce Brown did accept help
and she did admit to wanting to come indoors.

3.   To convince his readers of the truth of his position, Main presents what he believes to be one of the myths
about homelessness, and follows it with an argument disprov-
ing that myth.

4.   Main uses an emotional appeal to argue his point.
He is convincing when he reminds his reader that homelessness could happen to anybody.

5.   Marcuse seems to be saying that homelessness will
always be a factor in our "system" since the system is
working as it must. We cannot make accommodations for the
homeless because that may deplete efforts of greater social
importance.

6.   Main argues that homelessness is not a result of
decreased housing and that, in fact, the amount of available
housing has increased. However, landlords and developers
find it hard to comply with the federal and state regula-
tions for low-income housing. Main's apparent familiarity
with the subject convinces the reader of his argument. Many
students will agree that landlords and government agencies
must work together with homeless advocates to make more
affordable housing available.

Writing Topics (p. 758)

1.   You may want to remind students that not only is it
important to determine the ways in which the authors' styles
are the same, but also their topics. Since a topic may
dictate which tone or form of argument an author uses,
students should determine what the topics of "illiteracy"
and "homelessness" have in common.

2.   Students may wish to read more about the Ryan White
story before beginning this assignment. As the students
formulate their ideas they should keep the following in
mind: did Ryan White's battle against discrimination change
the views of society about AIDS and children with AIDS? How
important has Ryan's story been in educating the nation
about AIDS? Answering these questions may help students
understand society's position on AIDS and help students
organize their thoughts for an essay.

ABORTION IS TOO COMPLEX TO FEEL ALL ONE WAY ABOUT

Anna Quindlen

Questions for Study and Discussion (p. 761)

1.   The stories Quindlen tells at the beginning of her
essay are effective because they immediately set up for the
reader the limits and nature of Quindlen's dilemma in the
emotional, compassionate tone she will use throughout her
essay.

2. Quindlen's beliefs that "it is the right thing in some places and times," "the issue of abortion is difficult for all thoughtful people," and "legally I want always to have that right," have in common a concern for the men and women who face the decision to have an abortion. Her uncertainty over whether "a woman's right to choose is absolute," and her doubt that the unborn child is "a little blob of formless protoplasm," reflect her awareness of and compassion for the unborn child.

3. Since experiencing pregnancy and childbirth, Quindlen is no longer certain that a woman has the moral right to abort a pregnancy under any and all circumstances.

4. Some students will argue that Quindlen, who has wealth and a supportive mate, is not representative of many women facing abortion. Even though Quindlen makes that point herself, her position may still strike some readers as luxurious. On the other hand, some students may argue that it is precisely and only those who have been pregnant who can authentically address the issue of abortion.

5. Quindlen groups herself with the "thoughtful," those for whom there are no easy answers or absolutes in the question of abortion. She reveals a marked animosity and disdain for the "anti-abortionists," whom she describes as "smug and sometimes violent" and fanatical in nature. Quindlen is easier on the supporters of abortion rights (among whom she still counts herself), although she does chastise them for taking a "monolithic position" against the anti-abortionists.

6. Quindlen's audience, readers of the <u>New York Times</u>, are educated, sophisticated, and liberal. She risks offending a readership whom she must assume will tend to be pro-choice. However, she has strong feelings on the subject and has developed insights that will possibly de-polarize the abortion debate, a "closet" wish for many "thoughtful" people. Quindlen is counting on the fact that her audience will listen to her argument since she has established liberal credentials of her own.

Writing Topics (p. 762)

1. Before students begin work on this assignment it may be helpful to analyze with them examples of letters written to the editorial page of a local newspaper. Consider each in terms of its construction as an argument, noting especially the selection and organization of supporting evidence. You can also examine other features related to successful arguments as they are outlined under the following headings in the Glossary: ARGUMENT, DEDUCTION, INDUCTION, LOGICAL FALLACIES, and PERSUASION. After reviewing these concepts and applying them to sample letters, students may be better equipped to write a rebuttal to an article dealing with a controversial social issue.

2. The easiest way to approach this assignment would be to have the students write their essay with an epilogue

discussing the ease or difficulty they had writing their emotional essays. You may want to remind students that tone, and diction will be very important for the body of the essay. Students may review the Glossary entries at the back of the book for TONE and DICTION. The epilogues may be interesting to share with the class when the assignment is done.

CIVIL DISOBEDIENCE: DESTROYER OF DEMOCRACY

Lewis H. Van Dusen, Jr.

Questions for Study and Discussion (p. 769)

1. True civil disobedients break the law openly, nonviolently, without sacrificing others' rights and they stand ready to accept the penalty of their actions without resistance.

2. Injustice can be addressed through "persuasion of Congress and other legislative bodies and by the decision of courts" (14). Civil disobedience is acceptable in terms of an organized, peaceful, free assembly that does not infringe upon the rights of others.

3. By making a distinction between the "authentic" and "inauthentic" civil disobedient, Van Dusen achieves two things. First, in dispelling all possible "what ifs" in the mind of the reader, he eliminates disagreement with his argument. Secondly, by covering all aspects of civil disobedience, he lays the groundwork for his argument in favor of civil obedience.

4. Van Dusen surprises the reader with his less than flattering references to thinkers who hold places of honor in history and in our culture. By taking on men such as Thoreau, Gandhi, and Socrates, Van Dusen bravely demonstrates his adamant belief in his position. Students will either admire or scorn this kind of courage depending on how effectively they think Van Dusen has defended his position or how strongly they admire the thinkers he challenges.

5. The irony of taking the law into one's own hands is that the civil disobedient is proclaiming the unworkability of the democracy he or she claims to defend.

6. Van Dusen's tone is adamant and sometimes charged. He does not shirk from calling a spade a spade as is evident in his use of words such as: <u>violence</u>, <u>mop power</u>, <u>anarchy</u>, <u>bigoted chauvinist</u>, and <u>extort</u>. Students will find countless examples of Van Dusen's tough language.

7. Van Dusen claims that allowing civil disobedients to continue with their actions will inspire others to take such action. This will lead to the dangerous and widespread belief that democracy is unworkable. Some students will agree with Van Dusen that the system allows for the redress of wrongs. Others will argue that it is naive to expect

justice from a government they perceive as corrupt and out-of-reach.

8. Van Dusen foresees a widespread acceptance of civil disobedience leading to "an authoritarian or anarchic state."

Writing Topics (p. 769)

1. As a prewriting activity you may want to discuss the idea of civil disobedience in class and have students analyze Van Dusen's position on the topic as well as their own. This will help students decide whether they side with Van Dusen or not.

2. It may be interesting to have the students make speculations on how the differences and similarities are a product of the author's time. Both authors discuss the same topic, but a century separates the lives of the two authors.

3. You may wish to have students determine why college students protest. Is it because they are introduced to new people who have different concerns, or that they are introduced to problems they were never exposed to in high school, or is it simply their age that makes them interested in such protests?

ACTIVE AND PASSIVE EUTHANASIA

James Rachels

Questions for Study and Discussion (p. 777)

1. Rachels's thesis is that there is no meaningful moral distinction between active euthanasia--killing terminally ill or injured patients--and passive euthanasia--letting them die of their disabilities (1). Nowhere in the essay does he actually support euthanasia of either kind, and the sordid example he chooses to give in paragraphs 10-12 hints that he may actually be against euthanasia, since it introduces an otherwise gratuitously ugly note into his discussion.

2. To supplement the answer to #1 above, we would add that the most substantial difference Rachels discusses is that passive euthanasia may often permit a much more prolonged and painful death than would active euthanasia (3-4), so that active euthanasia may actually be the more human. However, it is also against the law (19) and against the American Medical Association's ethical standards (1), and people in general consider it less ethical.

3. The example of the child with Down's syndrome is not directly relevant to the issue because as Rachels points out in paragraph 6, an operation that is "not prohibitively difficult" would save the baby's life. Rather, the parents have decided that living with Down's syndrome will be worse for their child (or for them) than if the child died, and so

154

they permit it to die from an unrelated and remediable defect. (See S. I. Hayakawa, "Our Son Mark," page 111, for what might have happened had the child been saved.) Rachels includes this example partly to make more clear by negation what passive euthanasia is, and partly to include the poignant image of a tiny baby dying in needlessly prolonged pain.

4. The Smith-Jones case tests Rachels's claim that there is no moral difference between killing and letting die, and prepares for his discussion in paragraph 15 of why so many think there _is_ a moral difference. Creating a hypothetical example allows Rachels to determine fully the specific points of the comparison he wants to make; in real life, exactly parallel situations like the Smith-Jones case rarely occur. However, the example's strength is also its weakness, as some readers may find it contrived and unconvincing.

5. Rachels wrote his article to convince doctors in general, and those who write the AMA's ethical pronouncements, that they should reconsider the view that active euthanasia is "'contrary to that for which the medical profession stands'" whereas passive euthanasia is up to "'the patient and/or his immediate family'" to decide (1). His expected readers are doctors, as we know partly from the essay's source (The New England Journal of Medicine) and partly from the last sentence of paragraph 1. But obviously the article is understandable by and relevant to a general audience.

Writing Topics (p. 777)

1. Since the law and the AMA do permit passive euthanasia in some instances, this is not a wholly hypothetical question, but it is probably a question which few students have thought about--at least until they read Rachels's essay. Euthanasia approved or asked for by the patient is tantamount to suicide, so students may wish to approach this assignment from the perspective of the moral implications for someone choosing to die, and for someone deciding to let someone else die. The distinctions they see, if any, between these two areas of this topic may reveal something about their attitudes toward active versus passive euthanasia.

2. Sources for research into euthanasia can be found in the library under the heading Euthanasia.

3. This question moves from the issue of euthanasia to a far broader question, one that can be examined from many points of view and using many cases in point--most obviously the "Noble Experiment" of Prohibition. In the broadest sense, however, the purpose of law is to enforce certain moral and ethical rules that grow out of a society's needs and values. To make any act a crime, for example, is nothing if not a legislated moral judgment. The tension between law and morality is greatest, we think, when an act is

somehow classified as a crime when much or even most of a society does not believe that act to be immoral or unethical.

THE LOTTERY

Shirley Jackson

Questions for Study and Discussion (p. 785)

1. The first hint that there is something sinister about the lottery occurs in paragraph 43 when Tessie yells out nervously that her husband did not have enough time to draw. The family is not happy about being the chosen one. If readers remember the children making piles of stones, they may guess what the lottery is. By paragraph 75, the reader is sure that Tessie will be stoned.

2. Jackson uses matter-of-fact description to present "normality." She describes a day that is beautiful, "the flowers were blossoming profusely and the grass was richly green," not unlike other days. The lottery would only take two hours and everyone would be home in time for lunch. Tessie even forgot what day it was, because it was like any other day. The children are playing and the townspeople are joking. This air of normality contributes to the horror.

3. The ritual occurs every June 27th when the towns-people gather on the green and the man of the family picks a slip of paper for each family member from a black box. Once the family is chosen, all members give back their slips and redraw. The person with a black dot is stoned. The terrible irony is that no one remembers "why" they stone one of their neighbors to death every year.

4. Old Man Warner represents the conservative, tradi-tionalist view that what was good enough for the past is good enough for the future. He sees nothing but trouble in changing the old ways. Mr. Summers is thoroughly official from beginning to end. His job is to see that the lottery runs smoothly, not to consider its meaning. Nancy's friends, like Tessie, are passive until one of their own is threatened. They and Tessie probably represent the majority of the townspeople in their views.

5. The horror of the story is that Jackson's descrip-tion of the event is not unbelievable. The town is a small, ordinary town with ordinary daily routines and inhabitants. The characters are as average as is the setting.

6. The townspeople do not want to challenge tradition, although they do not recall its origins. The point that Jackson is making is that the group can be dangerous for its unwillingness to examine its actions or the consequences of those actions. The town is a metaphor for our culture, which has ceased to question the reasons for its behavior.

Writing Topics (p. 786)

1. As a prewriting activity it may be important to define <u>scapegoat</u> and discuss how it relates to this essay. With the definition in mind, students can research other scapegoat rituals and the cultures that practiced the rituals.

2. After students have completed this assignment you can share the results with them in regard to the range of rituals identified in the essays. You may find a consistency in the kinds of rituals the students decided to discuss, or you may discover some unique and interesting cases. Whatever the result of your analysis, your discussion can give students a more comprehensive look at the role ritual plays in our family lives.

The St. Martin's Guide to Writing

Third Edition

RISE B. AXELROD, California State University, San Bernardino
CHARLES R. COOPER, University of California, San Diego

A comprehensive rhetoric, reader, and handbook for freshman composition, *The St. Martin's Guide to Writing* was the first textbook to bring the writing process successfully into the classroom. Because it also provides thorough coverage of traditional rhetoric, instructors have complete flexibility to draw from both the old and the new. What sets this text apart from most other texts of its kind are its guides to writing, which escort students through the process of composing nine types of college discourse, and its systematic integration of reading and writing. In this new edition, the *Guide* continues its tradition of making important new methodology usable, providing a variety of tools for bringing collaborative learning into the classroom. Specifically new are: more than 50 specially-designed classroom activities, many suitable for small-group work; 21 of the essays and a brief anthology of stories; complimentary word-processing software that makes the writing guides available on disk; an anthology of essays done by students across the nation using the *Guide*; and, for instructors, a guide to evaluating student writing. In addition, the book has a new three-color design, with marginal cross-referencing to specific page numbers, to make it easier for students to use.

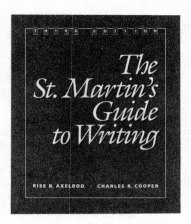

Hardcover. 720 pages (probable). 1991
ISBN: 0-312-03495-4

Accompanied by *The St. Martin's MindWriter and Descant*, a software program for invention and revision, and *The St. Martin's Hotline: Documentation Guide* (both available for both IBM and MacIntosh); *A Guide to Evaluating Student Writing;* an anthology of writing by students; and an *Instructor's Resource Manual*

The St. Martin's Guide to Writing

Short Third Edition

RISE B. AXELROD, California State University, San Bernardino
CHARLES R. COOPER, University of California, San Diego

Includes all the material in the Third Edition except for the handbook section.

Paperbound. 611 pages (probable). 1991
ISBN: 0-312-03494-6
See above listing for complete ancillary package.

Literature

150 MASTERPIECES OF FICTION, POETRY, AND DRAMA

Edited by BEVERLY LAWN, Adelphi University

An anthology of 150 masterpieces of literature —40 stories, 100 poems, and 10 plays— chosen for their enduring literary quality as well as their teachability and interest to students. A careful mix of "canonical" figures and fresh new voices, In addition to a broad selection of classics considered indispensable to a knowledge and appreciation of our literary heritage, *Literature: 150 Masterpieces* also presents important contemporary works by men and women of international interest and cultural insight. Professor Lawn provides a General Introduction and introductory essays for each of the genres; a concluding essay on writing about literature; and a glossary of literary terms illustrated with examples taken only from selections included in the anthology.

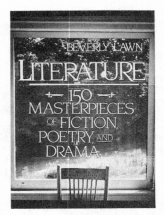

Introduction to Literature

Fiction: Introduction to Fiction • Nathaniel Hawthorne, Young Goodman Brown; Edgar Allan Poe, The Cask of Amontillado; Feodor Dostoevsky, A Christmas Tree and a Wedding; Leo Tolstoy, How Much Land Does a Man Need?; Sarah Orne Jewett, A White Heron; Guy de Maupassant, The Piece of String; Kate Chopin, The Story of an Hour; Stephen Crane, The Bride Comes to Yellow Sky; Sherwood Anderson, Death in the Woods; Arcadii Averchenko, The Young Man Who Flew Past; James Joyce, Araby; Franz Kafka, The Judgment; D.H. Lawrence, The Blind Man; Katherine Mansfield, The Doll's House; Katherine Anne Porter, Rope; William Faulkner, A Rose for Emily; Ernest Hemingway, A Clean, Well-Lighted Place; Langston Hughes, Thank You, M'am; James T. Farrell, The Benefits of American Life; Isaac Bashevis Singer, Joy; Tommaso Landolfi, Wedding Night; Eudora Welty, A Worn Path; Tillie Olsen, I Stand Here Ironing; John Cheever, The Swimmer; Ralph Ellison, King of the Bingo Game; Bernard Malamud, A Jewbird; Peter Taylor, A Walled Garden; Grace Paley, A Conversation with My Father; Nadine Gordimer, Town

and Country Lovers; Flannery O'Connor, A Temple of the Holy Ghost; Gabriel García Márquez, A Very Old Man with Enormous Wings; Donald Barthelme, The King of Jazz; John Updike, Pygmalion; Estela Portillo Trambley, The Burning; Joyce Carol Oates, The Girl; Toni Cade Bambara, The Lesson; Raymond Carver, The Third Thing That Killed My Father Off; Alice Walker, Roselily; Ann Beattie, Tuesday Night; Jayne Anne Phillips, Cheers

Poetry: Introduction to Poetry • Anonymous, Western Wind / Edward; Sir Walter Raleigh, The Nymph's Reply to the Shepherd; Sir Philip Sidney, With how sad steps, oh moon, thou climb'st the skies; Christopher Marlowe, The Passionate Shepherd to His Love; William Shakespeare, Sonnet 18 (Shall I compare thee to a summer's day?) / Sonnet 130 (My mistress' eyes are nothing like the sun); John Donne, The Bait / Batter my heart, three-person'd God; Robert Herrick, Delight in Disorder / To the Virgins, to Make Much of Time; George Herbert, Easter Wings; John Milton, When I consider how my light is spent; Richard Lovelace, To Lucasta, Going to the Wars,; Andrew Marvell, To His Coy Mistress; Henry Vaughan, The Retreat; John Dryden, A Song for St. Cecilia's Day; Jonathan Swift, A Description of the Morning; William Blake, London / The Garden of love; William Wordsworth, A Slumber Did My Spirit Seal; Samuel Taylor Coleridge, Kubla Khan; George Gordon, Lord Byron, She Walks in Beauty; Percy Bysshe Shelley, Ode to the West Wind / Ozymandias; John Keats, Ode on a Grecian Urn / To Autumn; Elizabeth Barrett Browning, If thou must love me, let it be for nought; Alfred, Lord Tennyson, The Splendor Falls on Castle Walls; Robert Browning, My Last Duchess; Walt Whitman, A Noiseless Patient Spider / There Was a Child Went Forth; Matthew Arnold, Dover Beach; Emily Dickinson, After great pain a formal feeling comes / Because I could not stop for Death— / I heard a Fly buzz — when I died; Christina Rossetti, Song; Thomas Hardy, The Darkling Thrush / Neutral Tones; Gerard Manley Hopkins, God's Grandeur / Pied Beauty; A.E. Housman, Loveliest of Trees, the Cherry Now; William Butler Yeats, Sailing to Byzantium; The Second Coming; Robert Frost, Birches / The Road Not Taken; Amy Lowe, The Taxi; Wallace Stevens, Thirteen Ways of Looking at a Blackbird; William Carlos Williams, To Elsie; D.H. Lawrence, Kangaroo; Ezra Pound, In a Station of the Métro / The River-Merchant's wife: A Letter; H.D. (Hilda Doolittle), Oread; Marianne Moore, The Steeple-Jack; T.S. Eliot, The Love Song of J. Alfred Prufrock; Gabriela Mistral, Country That Is Missing; Edna St. Vincent Millay, Spring; e.e. cummings, Buffalo Bill's / my sweet old etcetera; Langston Hughes, Harlem / Night Funeral in Harlem; Pablo Neruda, The Clock Fallen into the Sea; W.H. Auden, Musée des Beaux Arts; Theodore Roethke, I Knew a Woman; Elizabeth Bishop, In the Waiting Room; Robert Hayden, Those Winter Sundays; David Ignatow, Did you know that hair is flying around the universe?; Randall Jarrell, The Woman at the Washington Zoo; Dylan Thomas, Do Not Go Gentle into That Good Night; Gwendolyn Brooks, The Mother / We Real Cool; Robert Lowell, The Picture / Water; Richard Wilbur, Love Calls Us to the Things of This World; James Dickey, The Lifeguard; Denise Levertov, The Dragon-Fly Mother; Louis Simpson, Walt Whitman at Bear Mountain; Robert Bly, For My Son Noah, Ten Years Old; Allen Ginsberg, A Supermarket in California; John Ashbery, Paradoxes and Oxymorons; Galway Kinnell, Vapor Trail Reflected in the Frog Pond; W.S. Merwin, A Door; James Wright, A Blessing; Philip Levine, Starlight; Anne Sexton, Two Hands; Adrienne Rich, Diving into the Wreck; Ted Hughes, The Thought-Fox; Sylvia Plath, Mary's Song / Morning Song; Mary Oliver, Poem for My Father's Ghost; Lucille Clifton, Miss Rosie; Margaret Atwood, Book of Ancestors / Game after Supper; Seamus Heaney, Digging; Sharon Olds, The Victims; Tess Gallagher, The Sky Behind It; Philip Schultz, My Guardian Angel Stein; Carolyn Forché, The Colonel; Garrett Kaoru Hongo, Who Among You Knows the Essence of Garlic?; Jimmy Santiago Baca, Cloudy Day

Drama: Introduction to Drama • Sophocles, Oedipus Rex; William Shakespeare, Hamlet; Henrik Ibsen, A Doll's House; Anton Chekhov, A Marriage Proposal; Susan Glaspell, Trifles; John Millington Synge, Riders to the Sea; Tennessee Williams, The Glass Menagerie; Eugene Ionesco, The Lesson; Ed Bullins, A Son, Come Home; Marsha Norman, 'night, Mother

Writing about Literature
Glossary

Paperbound. 900 pages (probable). 1991
ISBN: 0-312-02357-X
Instructor's Manual available

Writing from Sources

Third Edition

BRENDA SPATT, Office of Academic Affairs,
City University of New York

A comprehensive text that teaches the skills
students need to write successfully from
sources—the basic techniques of comprehension, analysis, and synthesis that are common to all kinds of academic writing. A wealth
of readings from diversified sources, with
accompanying exercises, gives students
practice at every stage of the writing process,
as they progress from the single-source essay
to the multiple-source essay to the full-scale
research essay.

Approximately half the readings are new to
this edition, and there is a new appendix that
provides ten readings (including three cross-
referenced from the text) on the subject of
the powers and responsibilities of the mass
media—a "ready-made" set of sources for a
research paper. In addition, the text has been
completely redesigned for greater ease of
use: italics and bulleted lists now help students identify important points; a second col-
or further highlights important material; lists
of guidelines now appear in easily identifiable
screened boxes; and text material has been
clearly differentiated throughout from readings, exercises, and assignments.

I. Making Your Sources Your Own: *Reading
for Understanding:* Underlining • Annotating
• Asking Questions • Drawing Inferences •
Outlining • Writing a Summary • *Presenting
Sources to Others:* Reasons for Quoting •
Using Quotations • Tailoring Quotations to Fit
Your Writing • Writing Citations • Integrating
Quotations into Your Paragraphs • Avoiding
Plagiarism • Paraphrasing • Paraphrasing in
Two Stages • Incorporating Paraphrase into
Your Essay • Presenting Sources: A Summary
of Preliminary Writing Skills

II. Writing from Sources: *The Single-Source
Essay:* Strategy One: Separating Source and
Self • Strategy Two: Interpreting What You
Summarize • Strategy Three: Using a Source
as the Starting Point for Your Essay • Planning
a Single-Source Essay • Writing a Single-
Source Essay • *The Multiple-Source Essay:*
Selecting Information for a Multiple-Source
Essay • Generalizing from Examples • Analyz-
ing Multiple Sources • Synthesizing Multiple
Sources • Organizing Multiple Sources •
Evaluating Sources • Writing a Synthesis
Essay • Citing Sources • The Limits of Syn-
thesis • Synthesis and Comparison • Supple-
mentary Exercises and Assignments

III. Writing the Research Essay: *Gathering
Materials at the Library: Bibliography:* Focus-
ing the Topic: Biographical and Historical
Subjects • Focusing the Topic: Contemporary
Issues • Compiling a Working Bibliography:
Locating Sources • Compiling a Working Bib-
liography: Recording Basic Information • Tak-
ing Notes about the Usefulness of Each Source
• *Gathering Materials at the Library: Evaluat-
ing Sources:* Learning More about Your
Sources • Selecting Sources That Work Well

Together • Integrating Your Selected Sources
• Evaluating Seven Sources: An Example •
*Gathering Materials at the Library: Taking
Notes:* Taking Good Notes • Taking Notes
from Abstract Sources • *Presenting the
Results of Your Research: Organizing and
Writing the Essay:* Taking Inventory and
Developiong a List of Topics • Cross-Refer-
encing • Integrating Your Sources into Para-
graphs • Providing a Clear Account of Your
Evidence • Doing Justice to Your Sources •
Integrating Your Sources: An Example •
Selecting Quotations • *Presenting the Re-
sults of Your Research: Acknowledging Your
Sources:* Acknowledging Your Sources • Pla-
giarism: Stealing Ideas • Plagiarism: Stealing
Words • Using Documentation • The Final
Bibliography • The Annotated Bibliography •
The Research Essay: Three Sample Research
Papers

**Appendix A. Some Useful Reference
Sources:** Guidelines for Using Reference
Works • General Encyclopedias • Specialized
Encyclopedias • General Indexes • Biograph-
ical Sources • Semispecialized Indexes and
Abstracts • Indexes and Abstracts for Pro-
fessional Studies • Indexes to Statistical
Compilations.

**Appendix B. Some Basic Forms for
Documentation:** New MLA Parenthetical
Documentation • Other Methods for
Documentation

**Appendix C. Readings for a
Research Essay**

Appendix D: Writing Essay Examinations:
Reading the Question • Planning and Devel-
oping the Essay • Analyzing an Essay and an
Essay Question • Answering the Question •
Introducing Your Topic • Presenting Your
Essay to the Reader

Paperbound. 544 pages (probable). 1991
ISBN: 0-312-03504-7
Instructor's Manual and computer software—
*The St. Martin's Hotline: Documentation
Guide*—available